RAYS OF VICTORY SERIES

∞∞∞∞∞∞∞∞∞ ♦ ♦ ♦ ♦ ♦ ∞∞∞∞∞∞∞∞∞

∞∞∞∞∞∞∞∞∞∞ ♦ ♦ ♦ ♦ ♦ ∞∞∞∞∞∞∞∞∞∞

RAYS OF VICTORY SERIES

𝒯his Book Belongs to:

_____

(Your Beautiful Name)

Jesus Christ in you is greater than the foul spirit of racism. Let His Footprints lead you to daily Victory over racism.

RAYS OF VICTORY SERIES

∞∞∞∞∞∞∞∞∞∞ ♦ ♦ ♦ ♦ ♦ ∞∞∞∞∞∞∞∞∞∞

150 SIGNPOSTS TO VICTORY OVER RACISM

(Volume 1)

Empowering Sign Posts for Victory Over Racism

∞∞∞∞∞∞∞∞∞∞ ♦ ♦ ♦ ♦ ♦ ∞∞∞∞∞∞∞∞∞∞

Excerpts from "Nailing Racism to the Cross"

∞∞∞∞∞∞∞∞∞∞ ♦ ♦ ♦ ♦ ♦ ∞∞∞∞∞∞∞∞∞∞

Dr. Jacyee Aniagolu-Johnson

First Paperback Edition

Edited by Chad Steenerson (www.christianeditor.net)
Also edited by Uché Aniagolu (Ebony WoodHouse Productions)

Editing Style:
Please note that the editing style presented in this book by the second editor, Uché Aniagolu, is meant to emphasize reverence of God, His Son Jesus Christ and His Holy Spirit. This editing style may differ from what you are accustomed to, but we chose it for the reason noted above.

Cover design by Marble Tower Publishing, LLC
Cover Image Source: Online Microsoft Clip Art Gallery (Open Source)
Inside Textbox Image Source: Online Microsoft Clip Art Gallery (Open Source)

First Paperback Edition
ISBN 978-1-937230-01-2

Printed in the United States of America by Marble Tower Publishing, LLC

Publisher's Cataloging-In-Publication Data
(Prepared by The Donohue Group, Inc.)

Aniagolu-Johnson, Jacyee.

  150 sign posts to victory over racism : empowering sign posts for victory over racism : excerpts from "Nailing racism to the cross" / Jacyee Aniagolu-Johnson. -- 1st pbk. ed.

  3 v. ; cm. -- (Rays of victory series)

  ISBN: 978-1-937230-01-2 (v. 1)
  ISBN: 978-1-937230-02-9 (v. 2)
  ISBN: 978-1-937230-03-6 (v. 3)

  1. Racism--Religious aspects--Christianity. 2. Spiritual warfare. 3. Christian life. I. Title. II. Title: Nailing racism to the cross.

BV4599.5.R33 A56 2011
270/.08

∞∞∞∞∞∞∞∞∞∞ ♦ ♦ ♦ ♦ ♦ ∞∞∞∞∞∞∞∞∞∞

"I will instruct you and teach you in the way you should go; I will guide you with My eye."

Psalms 32:8

∞∞∞∞∞∞∞∞∞∞ ♦ ♦ ♦ ♦ ♦ ∞∞∞∞∞∞∞∞∞∞

∞∞∞∞∞∞∞∞∞∞∞ ♦ ♦ ♦ ♦ ♦ ∞∞∞∞∞∞∞∞∞∞∞

"Racism is still with us, but it is up to us to prepare our children for what they have to meet, and, hopefully, we shall overcome."

Rosa Parks

(Communication at Howard University, 1998 – Published by Courtland Millo, October 26, 2005, Source: www.washingtonpost.com)

∞∞∞∞∞∞∞∞∞∞∞ ♦ ♦ ♦ ♦ ♦ ∞∞∞∞∞∞∞∞∞∞∞

∞∞∞∞∞∞∞∞∞∞ ♦ ♦ ♦ ♦ ♦ ∞∞∞∞∞∞∞∞∞∞

"The truth is that in the eyes of God, our race, ethnicity or nationality does not make us either superior or inferior to anyone or group of people. Our family lineage, education, wealth, social status, influence or any other factor or distinction, does not make us better than any other family; neither will anything we own or possess as individuals make us more acceptable to God than others. All men and women, regardless of race, ethnicity or nationality, are created equal in God's excellent Image, and in humanity and dignity. This is a simple and holy truth that racism can never change."

Jacyee Aniagolu-Johnson, PhD
(Excerpt from "Rays of Victory: Nailing Racism to the Cross")

∞∞∞∞∞∞∞∞∞∞ ♦ ♦ ♦ ♦ ♦ ∞∞∞∞∞∞∞∞∞∞

∞∞∞∞∞∞∞∞∞∞ ◆ ◆ ◆ ◆ ◆ ∞∞∞∞∞∞∞∞∞∞

Dedication

This book is dedicated to our heavenly Father, God Almighty—the God of justice, equity and all goodness enveloped in One—our only one and true living God, who offered us all the gift of eternal salvation through His Son, our Lord and Savior Jesus Christ.

To my dear dad, Justice Anthony Aniagolu and my mom, Lady Maria Aniagolu whom I love dearly and who first taught me about God, His profound love, mercy, faithfulness and grace, and His holy justice against any form of evil, wickedness, oppression and injustice.

To all those, regardless of race, ethnicity or nationality, who need God's brilliant rays of victory to deal with and overcome racial prejudice and discrimination—may your individual victory through God's beams of justice come speedily as you abide in God's Holy Word, annointing and presence through Jesus Christ.

∞∞∞∞∞∞∞∞∞∞ ◆ ◆ ◆ ◆ ◆ ∞∞∞∞∞∞∞∞∞∞

∞∞∞∞∞∞∞∞∞∞ ♦ ♦ ♦ ♦ ∞∞∞∞∞∞∞∞∞∞

Acknowledgement

My foremost gratitude is to God my Heavenly Father for His Gift of Salvation through my Lord and Savior Jesus Christ, and His Holy Spirit Who dwells within me. It is He Who inspires and fuels me daily to overcome any and all challenges, including my experiences with racial prejudice and discrimination.

My deepest gratitude goes to my dad, Justice Anthony Aniagolu and my mom, Lady Maria Aniagolu, for being the most amazing parents and irreplaceable gifts from God. I will forever remain grateful to God for finding me worthy to have such phenomenal persons as mom and dad. I love always!

My special thanks go to my husband, Lamonte, who remains my earthly rock of Gibraltar, and through whom God continues to teach me His expression of true and unconditional love that has no bounds.

My special gratitude also goes to my sister, Maryanne, a lovely woman of God—thank you for continuing to help me to better understand how to hear the true voice of God and how to spend endless quality time in God's Holy Presence through prayer, thanksgiving and worship. I love you very much.

To my sister Uché, I thank God for the sweet fragrance of Christ in you. You are an embodiment of servanthood—selfless sacrificial giving—it is the greatness of God in you through Jesus Christ that empowers you to humble yourself to serve others; I have no doubt that God will magnify His glory in your life through Jesus Christ. I love you very much.

To my sister Chi-Chi who's giving spirit surpasses anyone that I know—May Luke 6:38 remain like a wellspring within you and may God continue to bless you and enrich your life beyond your wildest imagination through Jesus Christ! I love you very much.

To my brother Kizito whose deep and genuine love for God helps me to stay focused on Matthew 6:33; may the power of God's Holy Word continue to promote you from faith to faith and from glory to glory, in the awesome Name of our Lord and Savior Jesus Christ. I love you very much.

To the rest of my family, Tony, Emeka, Chuka, Lolly and Nwachu, I remain forever grateful to God for your lives, individual families and accomplishments. It is my prayer that John 3:16 will be and remain alive in your hearts. I love you very much.

To my sisters in the Lord Jesus Christ, Chinwe Igwegbe-Lane, Nonye Igwegbe and Cathy Agada, thank you for all your prayers and support and powerful prophetic words that sustained me during the final birthing stage of the Rays of Victory book series. May our Heavenly Father continue to take you from faith to Faith and from glory to Glory, in the awesome Name of our Lord and Savior Jesus Christ!

To all my friends, prayer partners and the Ocean of Mercy prayer group in Cork, Ireland, who prayed for and with me for the success of this book and the entire Rays of Victory Series—may God continue to bless you immensely in the awesome Name of our Lord and Savior Jesus Christ!

Finally, to the Body of Jesus Christ (believers in Christ, God's true priests and ministers around the world), regardless of denomination, race or ethniicty, may God's favor and blessings always overflow in your lives as you continue to spread the good news of the Gospel of our Lord and Savior Jesus Christ, and further His powerful ministry, all of which are firmly rooted in true and pure love, which is God Himself.

∞∞∞∞∞∞∞∞∞∞ ♦ ♦ ♦ ♦ ∞∞∞∞∞∞∞∞∞∞

Contents

∞∞∞∞∞∞∞∞∞∞∞ ◆ ◆ ◆ ◆ ◆ ∞∞∞∞∞∞∞∞∞∞∞

What is Racism?

"A situation in which one race maintains supremacy over another race through a set of attitudes, behaviors, social structures and ideologies. It involves four essential and interconnected elements:

Power: *the capacity to make and enforce decisions is disproportionately or unfairly distributed.*

Resources: *unequal access to such resources as money, education, information, etc.*

Standards: *standards for appropriate behavior are ethnocentric, reflecting and privileging the norms and values of the dominant race/society.*

Problem: *involves defining "reality" by naming "the problem" incorrectly, and thus misplacing it."*

-- Women's Theological Center, Boston, MA, 1994

∞∞∞∞∞∞∞∞∞∞∞ ◆ ◆ ◆ ◆ ◆ ∞∞∞∞∞∞∞∞∞∞∞

∞∞∞∞∞∞∞∞∞∞∞ ♦ ♦ ♦ ♦ ♦ ∞∞∞∞∞∞∞∞∞∞∞

Definitions of Racism

"Any distinction, exclusion, restriction, or preference based on race, color, descent, or national or ethnic origin which has the purpose or effect of nullifying or impairing the recognition, enjoyment, or exercise, on equal footing, of human rights and fundamental freedoms in the political, economic, social, cultural, or any other field of public life."

-- The ICERD (International Convention on the Elimination of All Forms of Racial Discrimination)

∞∞∞∞∞∞∞∞∞∞∞ ♦ ♦ ♦ ♦ ♦ ∞∞∞∞∞∞∞∞∞∞∞

"Racism has not disappeared… we confront forms of racism that are covert or more complex…"

-- The International Council on Human Rights Policy

∞∞∞∞∞∞∞∞∞∞∞ ♦ ♦ ♦ ♦ ♦ ∞∞∞∞∞∞∞∞∞∞∞

"Racism involves physical, psychological, spiritual, and social control, exploitation and subjection of one race by another race…This means that racial discrimination and injustice are established, perpetuated and promot-

20

ed throughout every institution of society - economics, education, entertain-
ment, family, labor, law, politics, religion, science and war..."

-- Phavia Kujichagulia

(Recognizing and Resolving Racism: A Resource and Guide for
Humane Beings)

∞∞∞∞∞∞∞∞∞∞ ♦ ♦ ♦ ♦ ♦ ∞∞∞∞∞∞∞∞∞∞

"Racism - Racial prejudice and discrimination that are support-
ed by institutional power and authority. The critical element that
differentiates racism from prejudice and discrimination is the use
of institutional power and authority to support prejudices and
enforce discriminatory behaviors in systematic ways with far-
reaching outcomes and effects..."

-- Enid Lee, Deborah Menkart and Margo Okazawa-Rey (eds.)

(Beyond Heroes and Holidays: A Practical Guide to K-12 Anti-
Racist, Multicultural Education and Staff Development.)

∞∞∞∞∞∞∞∞∞∞ ♦ ♦ ♦ ♦ ♦ ∞∞∞∞∞∞∞∞∞∞

∞∞∞∞∞∞∞∞∞∞ ♦ ♦ ♦ ♦ ♦ ∞∞∞∞∞∞∞∞∞∞

The Reason for this Book

For every person, every child of God to know, understand and use the awesome power of God's Holy Word and His power within him or her through Jesus Christ to slay the goliath, racism, that they may encounter anywhere.

"You, dear children, are from God and have overcome them, because the one who is in you is greater than the one who is in the world."
1 John 4:4, NIV

∞∞∞∞∞∞∞∞∞∞ ♦ ♦ ♦ ♦ ♦ ∞∞∞∞∞∞∞∞∞∞

To receive the spirit of racism is to reject God's Holy Word.
To practice racism is to disobey God's Holy Word.
To reject the spirit of racism is to uphold God's Holy Word.

∞∞∞∞∞∞∞∞∞∞ ♦ ♦ ♦ ♦ ♦ ∞∞∞∞∞∞∞∞∞∞

∞∞∞∞∞∞∞∞∞ ♦ ♦ ♦ ♦ ♦ ∞∞∞∞∞∞∞∞∞

Preface

This book, "150 Sign Posts to Victory Over Racism-Volume 1," contains excerpts from the "Rays of Victory-Nailing Racism to the Cross" book series. The goal in writing this book is to lead you to accept Jesus Christ as your personal Lord and Savior, if you have not already done so; to guide you to God's holy truth in His Holy Word by the revelation power of His Holy Spirit; and for you to understand how to submit to God's Word and allow Him to unveil your natural eyes, replacing them with spiritual eyes through Jesus Christ. Then, with spiritual eyes you can begin to recognize the activities of the foul spirit of racism that is behind the racial prejudice and discrimination that you have experienced in the past or that you are currently experiencing. You will come to understand how racism attacks you and tries to intimidate you to submit to evil domination.

The father of racism has been cast out of God's Kingdom of truth and light because it was borne out of rebellion and disobedience to God (Revelation 12:7-12). The foul spirit of racism has been defeated and you have the power of Jesus Christ in you over it (Colossians 2:8-10; Matthew 28:18; Luke

10:18-19). So unless you grant it access to your soul, it has no legal authority in or over your life, for you are a child of the Most High God through Jesus Christ. The excerpts in this book will highlight Scripture that show you how not to submit to the obnoxious spirit of racism; rather, how to apply God's Holy Word, to identify and demolish the stranglehold that racism may have on your soul.

Daily, while the obnoxious spirit of racism may continue to try to gain access to your heart to rule you, you have the power and authority of the Sword of the Spirit, God's Holy Word, given to you by God through our Lord and Savior Jesus Christ, and the consuming fire of God's Holy Spirit—to pull down the stranglehold or iron grip of racism—to shatter the walls of racism—to dismantle the gates of racism—and to uproot, extract and destroy the hereditary line or family tree of racism (Jeremiah 1:10). You have God's power and anointing within you to break every yoke of the burden of racism (Isaiah 10:27). You have the power of the light and truth of God's Holy Word in you to plant within you new, fresh holy Seed of our Lord and Savior Jesus Christ that racism lacks the power to uproot or destroy.

If you have already allowed the foul spirit of racism access to your soul, now is the time to cast it out—or if you have not granted the evil spirit of racism any such access, keep the door to your soul permanently shut to it, with the power of the holy truth of God's awesome Word.

24

∞∞∞∞∞∞∞∞∞∞ ♦ ♦ ♦ ♦ ♦ ∞∞∞∞∞∞∞∞∞∞

Scripture Meditation

Let God battle those who oppress you—let God oppose those who oppose you—let Him be an Enemy to your enemies, and an Adversary to your adversaries (Exodus 23:22)— let Him manifest victory for you—the battle is not yours but the Lords'

- **1 Samuel 17:45-47**

∞∞∞∞∞∞∞∞∞∞ ♦ ♦ ♦ ♦ ♦ ∞∞∞∞∞∞∞∞∞∞

∞∞∞∞∞∞∞∞∞∞ ♦ ♦ ♦ ♦ ♦ ∞∞∞∞∞∞∞∞∞∞

How to Use this Book

This book contains empowering guideposts for your individual triumph over racism. During your quiet and serene moments, read and meditate on each excerpt, page by page, and most importantly, on God's Holy Word. To mediate means to reflect on or to contemplate; to look at attentively and thoughtfully; to consider carefully and at length or ponder; to have in mind as an intention or possibility.[1] So, like a fresh spring of water, let God's Holy Word running through the "sign posts" soak into your heart and mind and help you to begin to carve out a spiritual roadmap for you and become your daily Christ-rooted strategy for victory over racism. Let each excerpt help you to refocus your mind on God's Holy Word and its holy power to renew and fortify your mind against the foul spirit of racism (Romans 12:2).

Let the excerpts in this book become guiding sign posts that lead you to draw daily-renewed strength from God's Holy Scripture, through Jesus Christ and by the revelation power of God's Holy Spirit. Let the power of God's Holy Word and His amazing grace unshackle you forever from the invisible chains of racism.

First, let's profess Jesus Christ as our Lord and Savior, and receive the redeeming power of His precious Blood in our individual lives. For it is under the covering of the precious Blood of Jesus that we can receive the hidden power of God's Rays of Victory over racism (Habakkuk 3:4).

Chapter Reference

1. *www.thefreedictionary.com*

∞∞∞∞∞∞∞∞∞ ◆ ◆ ◆ ◆ ∞∞∞∞∞∞∞∞∞∞

∞∞∞∞∞∞∞∞∞∞ ♦ ♦ ♦ ♦ ♦ ∞∞∞∞∞∞∞∞∞∞

A Prayer of Salvation

On this day, _____, I,

_____ confess with my mouth that the Lord Jesus

Christ is my personal Savior; I believe that He shed His Blood

for me on the Cross of Calvary and that God raised Him from

the dead for my eternal salvation. I repent of my sins and ask

for God's forgiveness through the mighty Blood of Jesus Christ.

On this day, _____ by my faith, I,

_____ believe that I am now saved by the pre-

cious Blood of Jesus Christ. I believe in the Triune God: God

the Father, God's Son, Jesus Christ and God the Holy Spirit. I

believe that in the Name of our Lord and Savior JesusChrist, I

will receive the baptism of God's Holy Spirit that will release

from my heart the flowing rivers of Living Water, in Jesus'

Name, Amen.

Thank you Father, Lord God, for on this day,

_____, in the Name of Jesus Christ, I, _____ am

Born Again!

Scripture Meditation:

"For God so loved the world that He gave His Only Begotten Son, that whoever believes in Him should not perish but have everlasting life." – John 3:16

"But what does it say? 'The word is near you, in your mouth and in your heart' (that is, the word of faith which we preach): that if you   confess with your mouth the Lord Jesus and believe in your heart that God has raised Him from the dead, you will be saved. For with the heart one believes unto righteousness, and with the mouth confession is made unto salvation." – Romans 10:8-9

"He who believes in Me, as the Scripture has said, out of his heart will flow rivers of Living Water." – John 7:38

"That which is born of the flesh is flesh, and that which is born of The Spirit is spirit. Do not marvel that I said to you, 'You must be Born Again.'" – John 3:6-7

∞∞∞∞∞∞∞∞∞∞ ◆ ◆ ◆ ◆ ∞∞∞∞∞∞∞∞∞∞

A Prayer after Profession of Salvation

∞∞∞∞∞∞∞∞∞ ♦ ♦ ♦ ♦ ♦ ∞∞∞∞∞∞∞∞∞

Dear Glorious Heavenly Father, thank You that I am born again by the precious Blood of Jesus Christ. I accept my renewed spirit in Him.

Dear gracious Father, I thank You for making me aware that I have spiritual and mental shackles from my experiences with racism. Thank You for revealing to me all areas where I am shackled. Thank You for giving me total release and freedom from the intrigues of the foul spirit of racism. I reject the evil tradition of racism and all that it stands for. I forgive anyone who has hurt or offended me in any manner, including my racist offenders.

Dear precious Father, I believe that You have answered my prayers in the precious Name of Jesus Christ. In the Name of Jesus Christ and by Your enabling grace, Lord God, I know that I can and that I have gained victory over any form of racial oppression and injustice.

Thank You, awesome Father, for Your marvelous rays of victory over racism on my behalf, and for Your limitless and boundless power within me through Jesus Christ, Amen.

Scripture Meditation:

"And whatever you ask in My Name, I will do, that the Father may be Glorified in the Son. If you ask anything in My Name, I will do it." – John 14:13-14

"Pray without ceasing; in everything give thanks; for this is the Will of God in Jesus Christ for you." – 1 Thessalonians 5:17-18

"And whenever you stand praying, if you have anything against anyone, forgive him that your Father in Heaven may also forgive you your trespasses." – Mark 11:25

"Until now you have asked nothing in My Name. Ask and you will receive, that your joy may be full." – John 16:24

"Don't copy the behavior and customs of this world, but let God transform you into a new person by changing the way you think. Then you will learn to know God's Will for you, which is good and pleasing and perfect." – Romans 12:2

∞∞∞∞∞∞∞∞∞ ♦ ♦ ♦ ♦ ♦ ∞∞∞∞∞∞∞∞∞

Partnership Prayer

∞∞∞∞∞∞∞∞∞∞∞ ♦ ♦ ♦ ♦ ∞∞∞∞∞∞∞∞∞∞∞
♥

I commit to spending quality time in prayer, worship and thanksgiving, and meditating on God's Holy Word, to receive His powerful and winning strategies for my daily victory over racism. This I shall do only by the grace of God, in the Name of our Lord and Savior Jesus Christ and through daily guidance by the Holy Spirit. I stand in agreement with my prayer partner(s) _____ believing that through the redeeming precious Blood of Jesus Christ, God has taken away the burden of racism, its reproach and yoke of destruction from all areas of my life. I stand in agreement with my prayer partner(s) _____ believing that the precious Blood of Jesus Christ has permanently destroyed and removed the power of the burden of the foul spirit of racism in my life, in Jesus' Name, Amen.

_____
Your Name

_____
Prayer Partner's Name

∞∞∞∞∞∞∞∞∞∞∞ ◆ ◆ ◆ ◆ ∞∞∞∞∞∞∞∞∞∞∞

Jacyee Aniagolu Johnson

Dr. Jacyee Aniagolu-Johnson
(Author remains in agreement with you)

"Again I say to you that if two of you agree on earth concerning anything that they ask, it will be done for them by My Father in heaven." – Matthew 18:19

"It shall come to pass in that day that his burden will be taken away from your shoulder, and his yoke from your neck, and the yoke will be destroyed because of the anointing oil." – Isaiah 10:27

♥

∞∞∞∞∞∞∞∞∞∞∞ ◆ ◆ ◆ ◆ ◆ ∞∞∞∞∞∞∞∞∞∞∞

Introduction

∞∞∞∞∞∞∞∞∞∞ ♦ ♦ ♦ ♦ ♦ ∞∞∞∞∞∞∞∞∞∞∞

This book is about helping you to gain individual victory over racism; by standing in the victory that Jesus Christ gained for you on the Holy Cross, where He nailed your sins and every form of evil, wickedness, repression or oppression, including racism.

To stand in victory over racism, you must first come under the covering of the precious Blood of our Lord and Savior Jesus Christ. You need to accept Jesus Christ as your personal Lord and Savior. Once you have *truly* accepted and confessed Jesus Christ as your Redeemer, you are transformed into a new creation in Christ (2 Corinthians 5:17). You become "born again" in Christ—through Him you receive eternal salvation (John 3:6-7, 16; Romans 10:9-10). To be "born again" or "reborn" in Christ does not mean a physical rebirth but a spiritual renewal of your spirit.

To gain individual victory over racism or any other form of evil, you must first come to know and understand who you are in Christ. You are a child of God through the righteousness of Christ, an heir of God, and joint-heir with Christ (Romans 8:15-18). You are fearfully and wonderfully made, and you are an excellent product of His marvelous works (Psalms 139:13-14). So, you must come to see yourself as God sees you and not as prejudiced or racist individuals see you or present you to the world. You must start to meditate on God's Holy Word and allow it to begin to renew your mind daily through Jesus Christ (Romans 12:2) so that you do not allow lies of racism to distort your view or image of yourself.

The Oxford dictionary defines the word to "meditate" as to "focus one's mind for a period of time, in silence or with the aid of chanting…"[1] and God's Word which preceeds any dictionary definition instructed Joshua in the Book of Joshua 1:8 KJV (and instructs us now) to meditate on His Word when He said: "This book of the law shall not depart out of thy mouth; but thou shalt meditate therein day and night, that thou mayest observe to do according to all that is written therein: for then thou shalt make thy way prosperous, and then thou shalt have good success."

Therefore, it is clear that God wants us to not just read His Holy Word, but to also meditate on it and He stated the benefits: "for then thou shalt make thy way prosperous, and then thou shalt have good success." When you meditate on God's Word, it becomes planted and rooted in your heart and it soaks your mind and you begin to receive deeper revelation knowledge from His Holy Spirit about that Word; knowledge that is beyond the obvious meaning of the written (Logos) Word. Meditation on the Word causes it to spring up and forth in our heart and mind and becomes alive in us, and then its promises also become spiritually tangible. Truthfully, unless God's Word becomes real in your heart, it will not birth into victory in your physical environment. As my sister Uché once put it, unless God's Word becomes palpable in your heart, you will not reap its promises in a tangible way.

If you have already allowed racism to distort your discernment or view of your image of yourself in your mind, then you need to let God's Holy Word start the process of renewing your mind and give you a brand new view of your image in your mind—the authentic view of your image, which is your true spiritual image in Him. As a child of God, you cannot allow the foul spirit of racism to deceive you into believing lies that racism presents to you about who you are—because racism is of the devil who is the father of all lies and no truth can ever come from him (John 8:44); rather you are to veto and thrash the lies of racism, believe God's Word and obey His Word and do His will (James 1:22-25).

God's will is for you to silence the vile spirit of racism with the power of His Holy Word in you. You are what God's Word says you are and not what racists declare that you are. As a child of God you have God's power in you: Jesus Christ is in you and the Holy Spirit—to pull down every stranglehold or iron grip of racism and bring racism and its evils to submit to God's Holy Word (2 Corinthians 10:3-5).

Are you burdened by the foul spirit of racism and cannot seem to shake it off? Do you wish to turn over a new leaf with a life that is devoid of prejudiced feelings or racist actions? Are you a member of the huge "club" of individuals who face the daily storms of racism in the workplace or elsewhere? Have you had enough of the negative spiritual, mental or even physical abuse and torture by your experiences with racism? If you have, please come with me on this powerful trip with God's Spiritual knowledge, guidance and empowerment. Let the excerpts in is book, empowering "sign posts" guide you on how to draw daily-renewed strength from God's Holy Scripture. Let the power of God's Holy Word and His amazing grace unshackle you forever from the invisible chains of racism.

Now, let us begin a new journey with Jesus Christ—a renewed path of righteousness and holy power, faith, love, truth, holiness, mercy, forgiveness, charity and justice. Let us turn a new leaf and start a new and fabulous journey with Him that takes us to victory over daily challenges and obstacles—and over the foul and obnoxious spirit of racism. Are you ready to follow God's "Sign Posts to Victory Over Racism"? If you are, please turn to the next page!

Chapter Reference

[1] http://oxforddictionaries.com/definition/english/meditate

∞∞∞∞∞∞∞∞∞ ◆ ◆ ◆ ◆ ∞∞∞∞∞∞∞∞∞

"150 Sign Posts to Victory Over Racism – Volume 1" Begins:

1

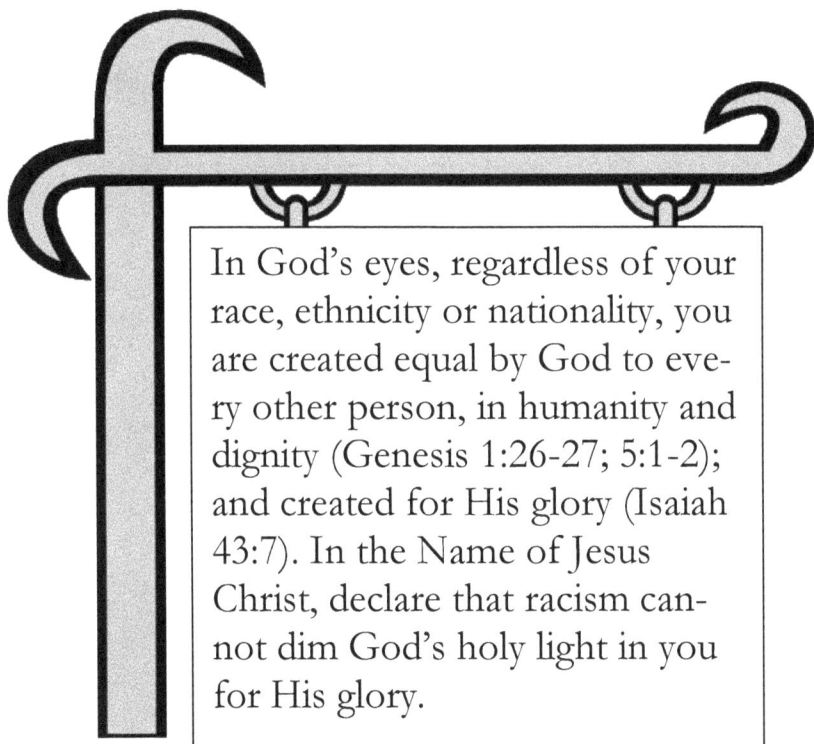

In God's eyes, regardless of your race, ethnicity or nationality, you are created equal by God to every other person, in humanity and dignity (Genesis 1:26-27; 5:1-2); and created for His glory (Isaiah 43:7). In the Name of Jesus Christ, declare that racism cannot dim God's holy light in you for His glory.

2

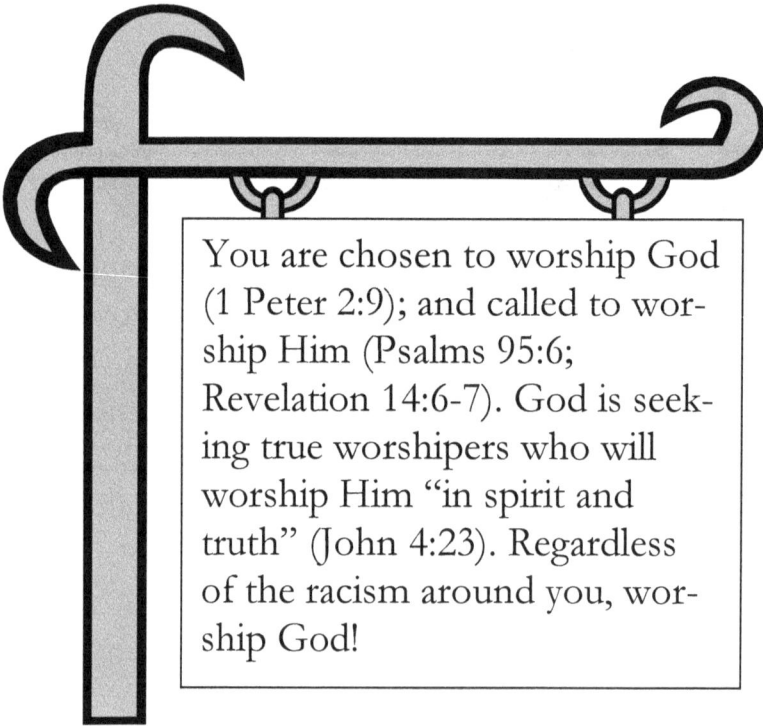

You are chosen to worship God (1 Peter 2:9); and called to worship Him (Psalms 95:6; Revelation 14:6-7). God is seeking true worshipers who will worship Him "in spirit and truth" (John 4:23). Regardless of the racism around you, worship God!

3

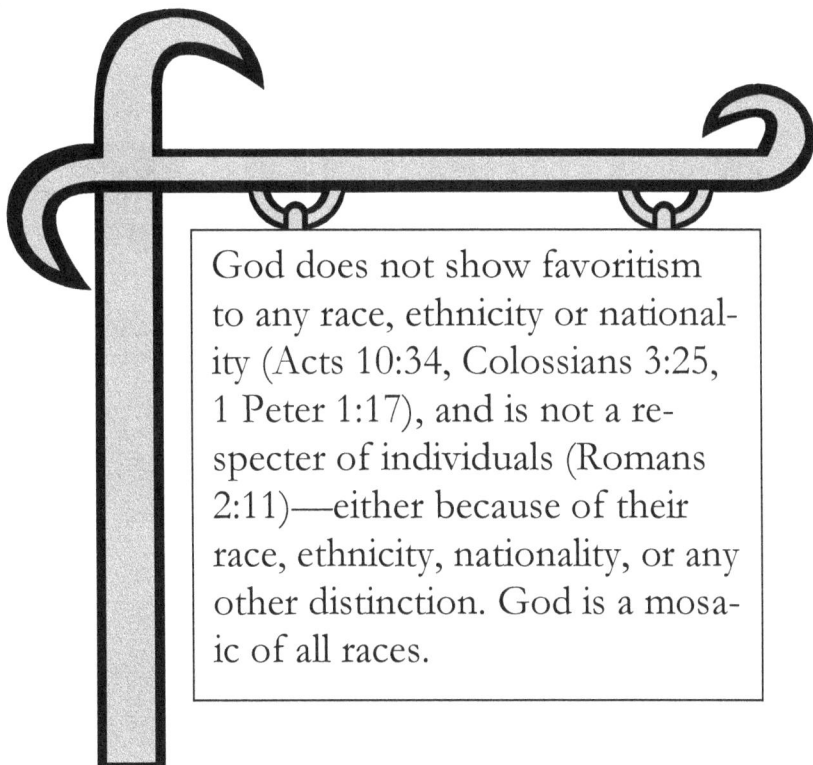

God does not show favoritism to any race, ethnicity or nationality (Acts 10:34, Colossians 3:25, 1 Peter 1:17), and is not a respecter of individuals (Romans 2:11)—either because of their race, ethnicity, nationality, or any other distinction. God is a mosaic of all races.

4

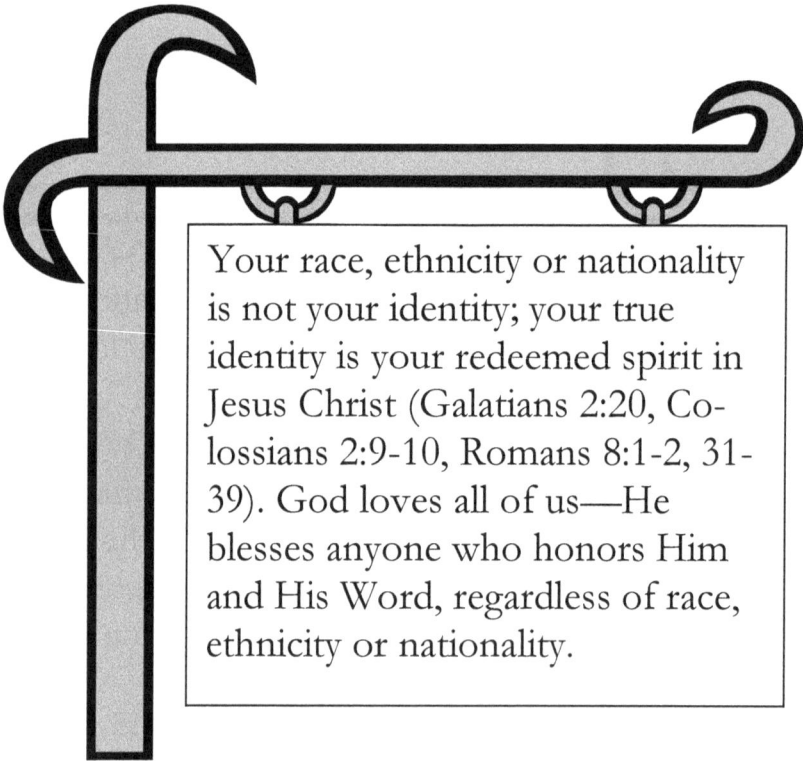

Your race, ethnicity or nationality is not your identity; your true identity is your redeemed spirit in Jesus Christ (Galatians 2:20, Colossians 2:9-10, Romans 8:1-2, 31-39). God loves all of us—He blesses anyone who honors Him and His Word, regardless of race, ethnicity or nationality.

5

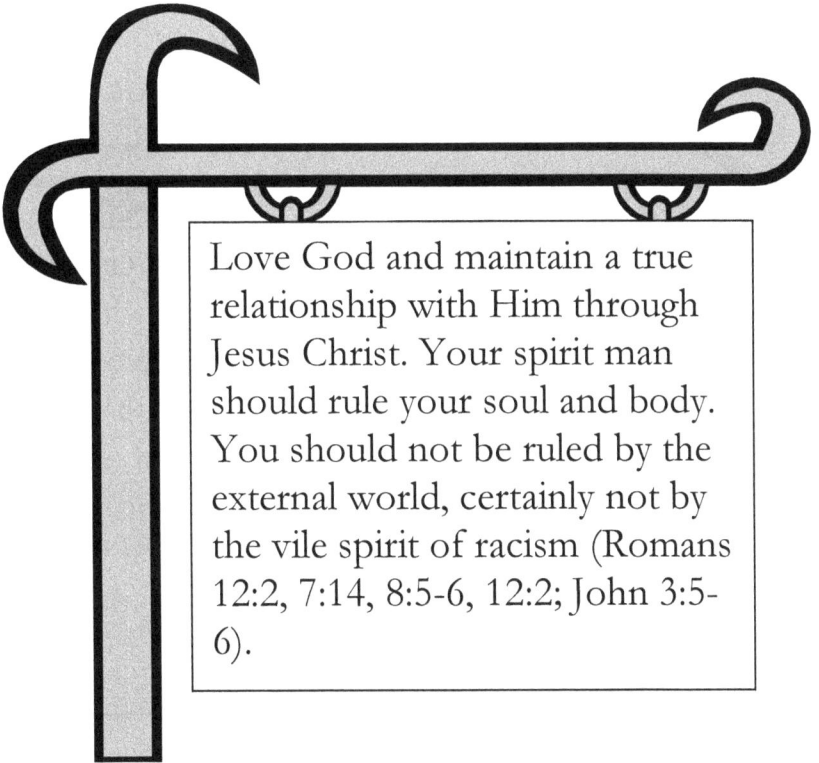

Love God and maintain a true relationship with Him through Jesus Christ. Your spirit man should rule your soul and body. You should not be ruled by the external world, certainly not by the vile spirit of racism (Romans 12:2, 7:14, 8:5-6, 12:2; John 3:5-6).

6

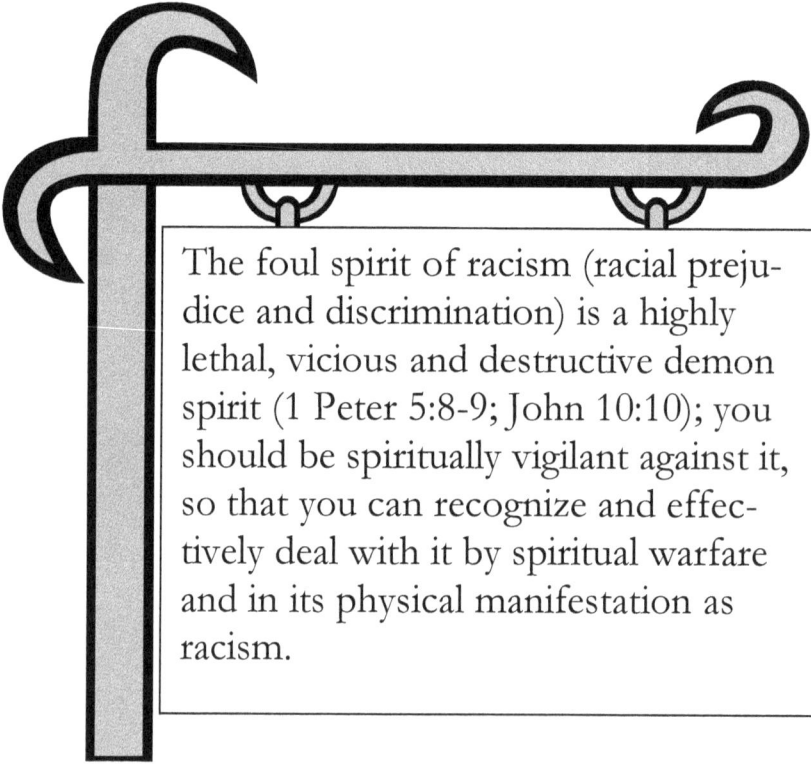

The foul spirit of racism (racial prejudice and discrimination) is a highly lethal, vicious and destructive demon spirit (1 Peter 5:8-9; John 10:10); you should be spiritually vigilant against it, so that you can recognize and effectively deal with it by spiritual warfare and in its physical manifestation as racism.

7

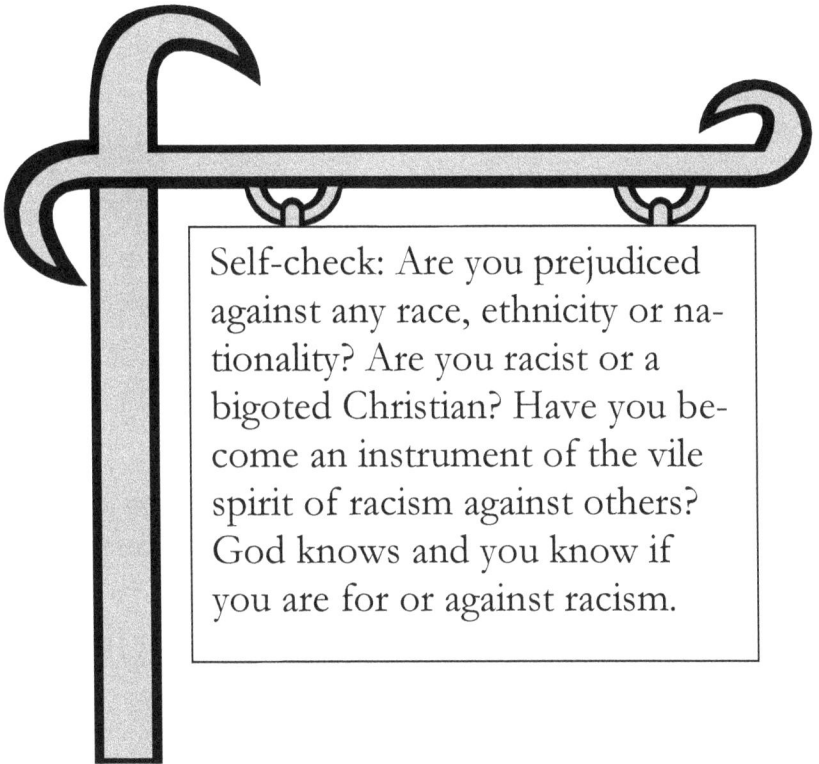

Self-check: Are you prejudiced against any race, ethnicity or nationality? Are you racist or a bigoted Christian? Have you become an instrument of the vile spirit of racism against others? God knows and you know if you are for or against racism.

8

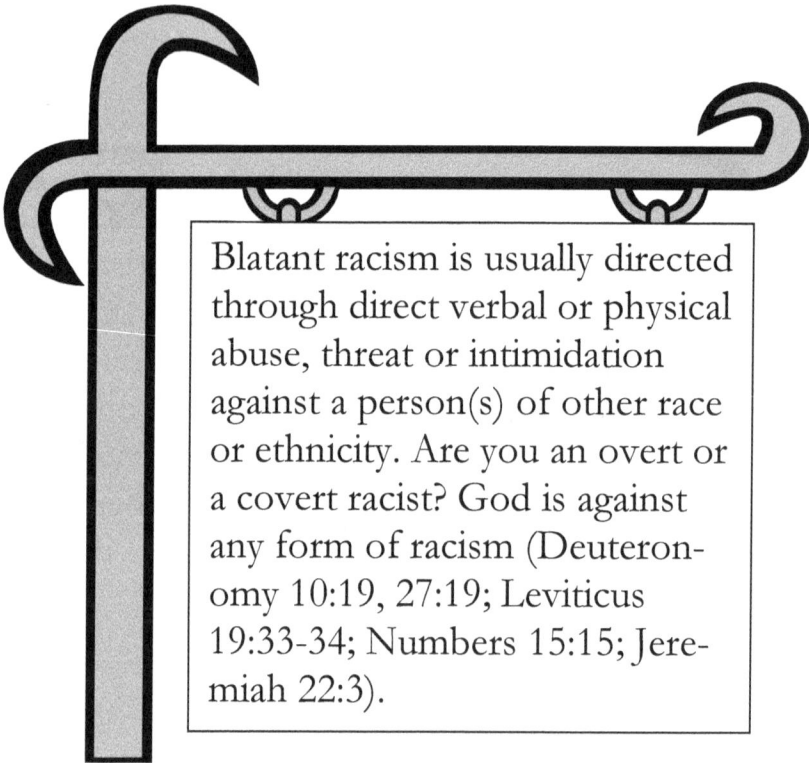

Blatant racism is usually directed through direct verbal or physical abuse, threat or intimidation against a person(s) of other race or ethnicity. Are you an overt or a covert racist? God is against any form of racism (Deuteronomy 10:19, 27:19; Leviticus 19:33-34; Numbers 15:15; Jeremiah 22:3).

9

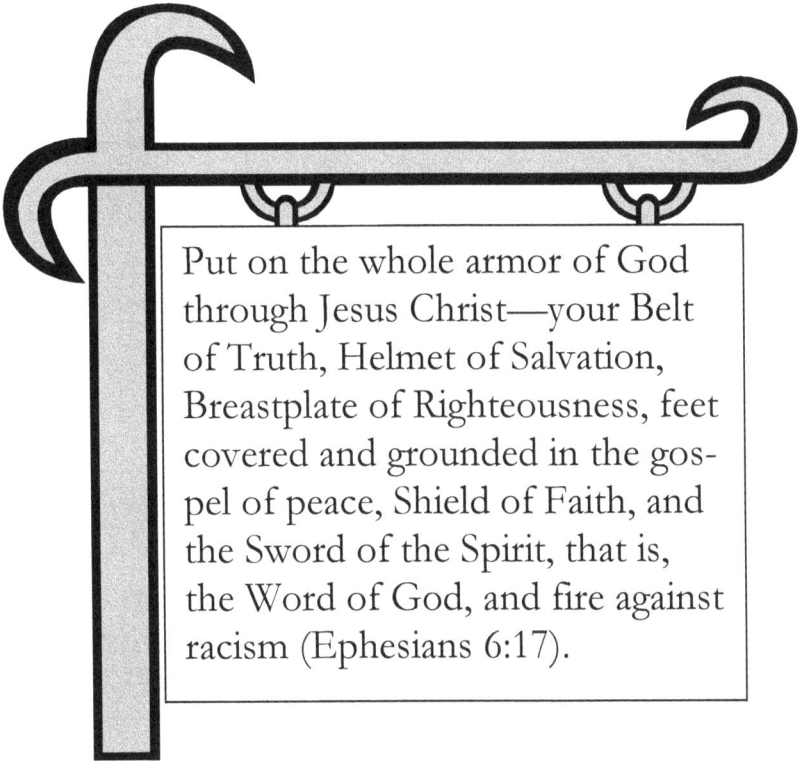

Put on the whole armor of God through Jesus Christ—your Belt of Truth, Helmet of Salvation, Breastplate of Righteousness, feet covered and grounded in the gospel of peace, Shield of Faith, and the Sword of the Spirit, that is, the Word of God, and fire against racism (Ephesians 6:17).

10

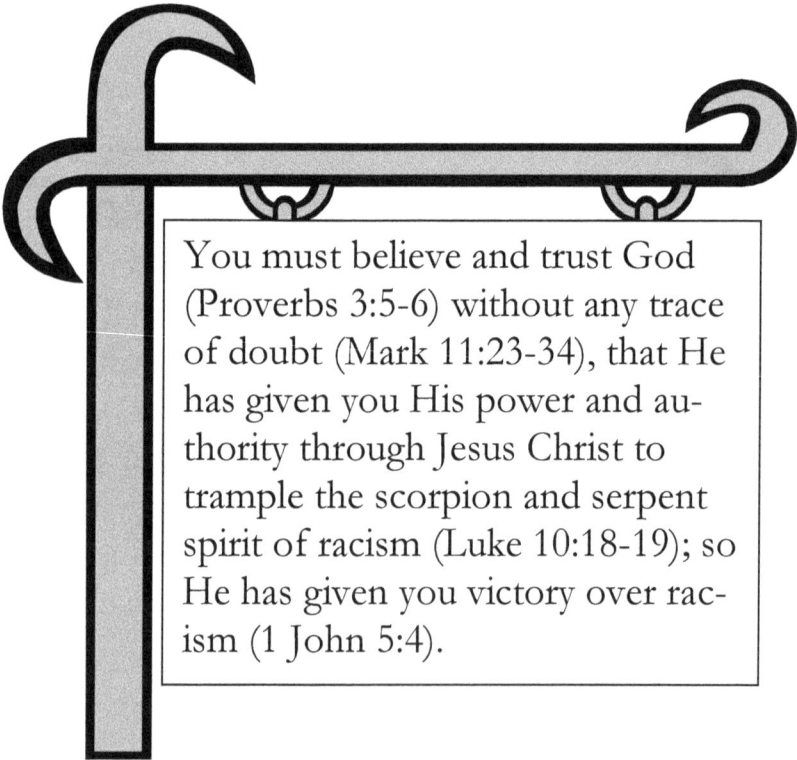

You must believe and trust God (Proverbs 3:5-6) without any trace of doubt (Mark 11:23-34), that He has given you His power and authority through Jesus Christ to trample the scorpion and serpent spirit of racism (Luke 10:18-19); so He has given you victory over racism (1 John 5:4).

11

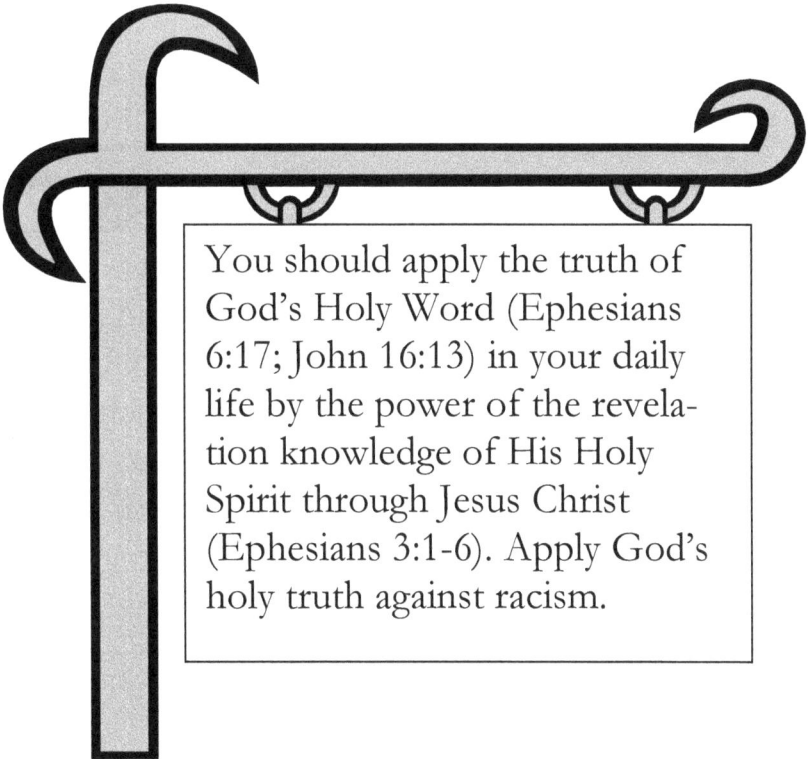

You should apply the truth of God's Holy Word (Ephesians 6:17; John 16:13) in your daily life by the power of the revelation knowledge of His Holy Spirit through Jesus Christ (Ephesians 3:1-6). Apply God's holy truth against racism.

12

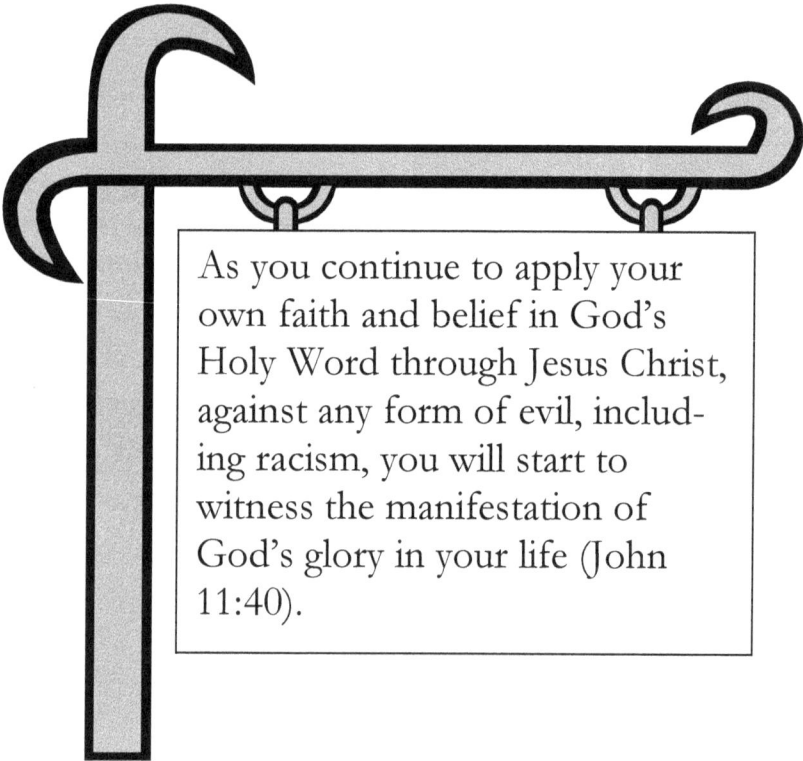

As you continue to apply your own faith and belief in God's Holy Word through Jesus Christ, against any form of evil, including racism, you will start to witness the manifestation of God's glory in your life (John 11:40).

13

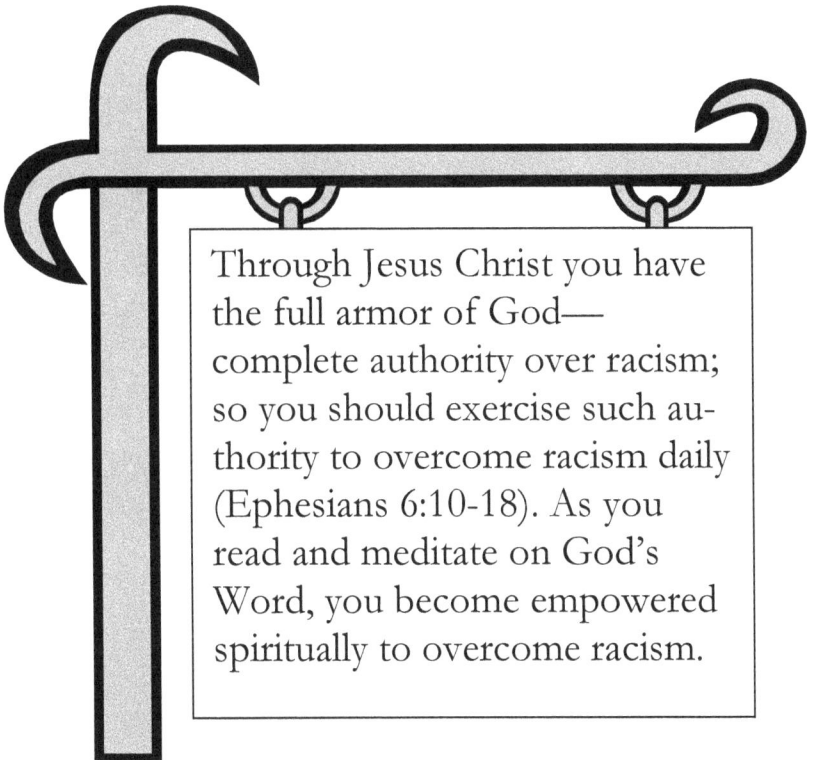

Through Jesus Christ you have the full armor of God—complete authority over racism; so you should exercise such authority to overcome racism daily (Ephesians 6:10-18). As you read and meditate on God's Word, you become empowered spiritually to overcome racism.

14

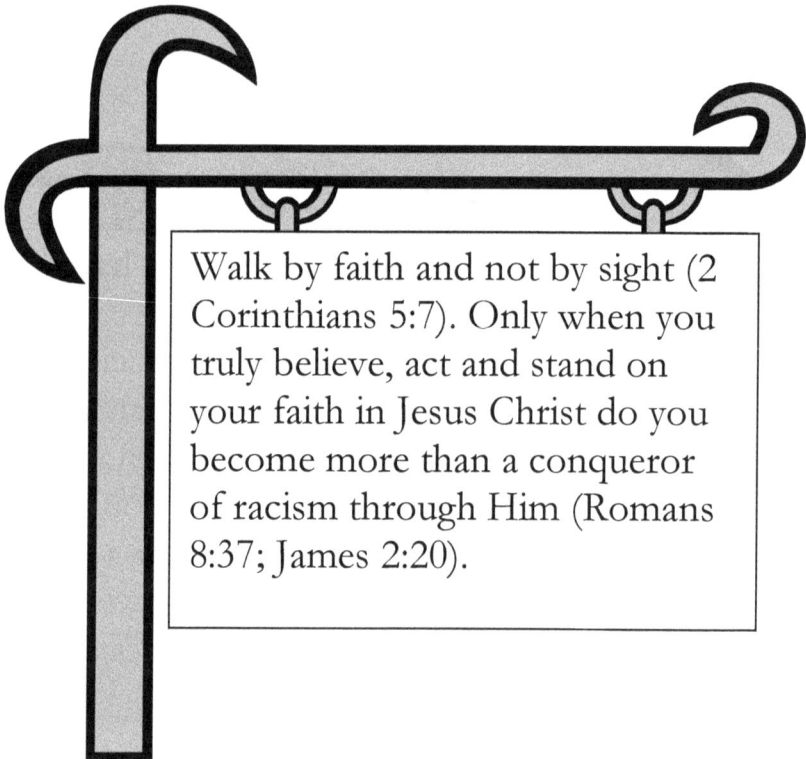

Walk by faith and not by sight (2 Corinthians 5:7). Only when you truly believe, act and stand on your faith in Jesus Christ do you become more than a conqueror of racism through Him (Romans 8:37; James 2:20).

15

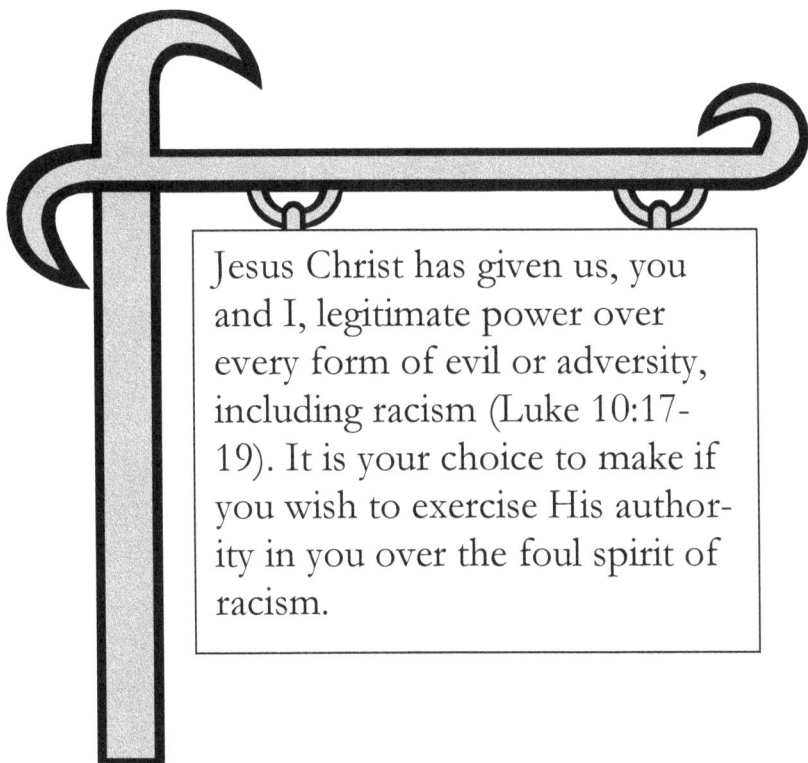

Jesus Christ has given us, you and I, legitimate power over every form of evil or adversity, including racism (Luke 10:17-19). It is your choice to make if you wish to exercise His authority in you over the foul spirit of racism.

16

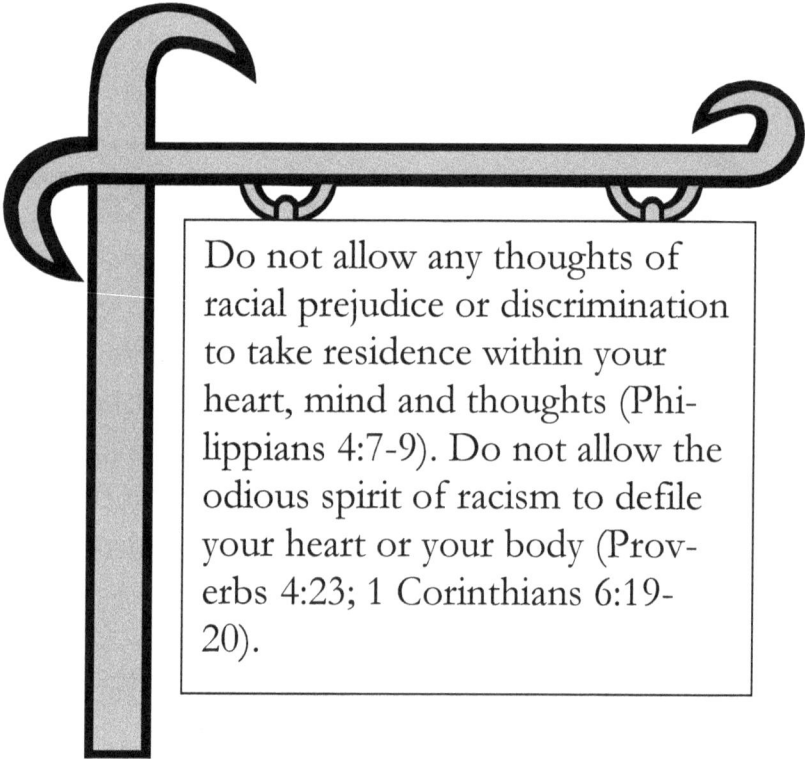

Do not allow any thoughts of racial prejudice or discrimination to take residence within your heart, mind and thoughts (Philippians 4:7-9). Do not allow the odious spirit of racism to defile your heart or your body (Proverbs 4:23; 1 Corinthians 6:19-20).

17

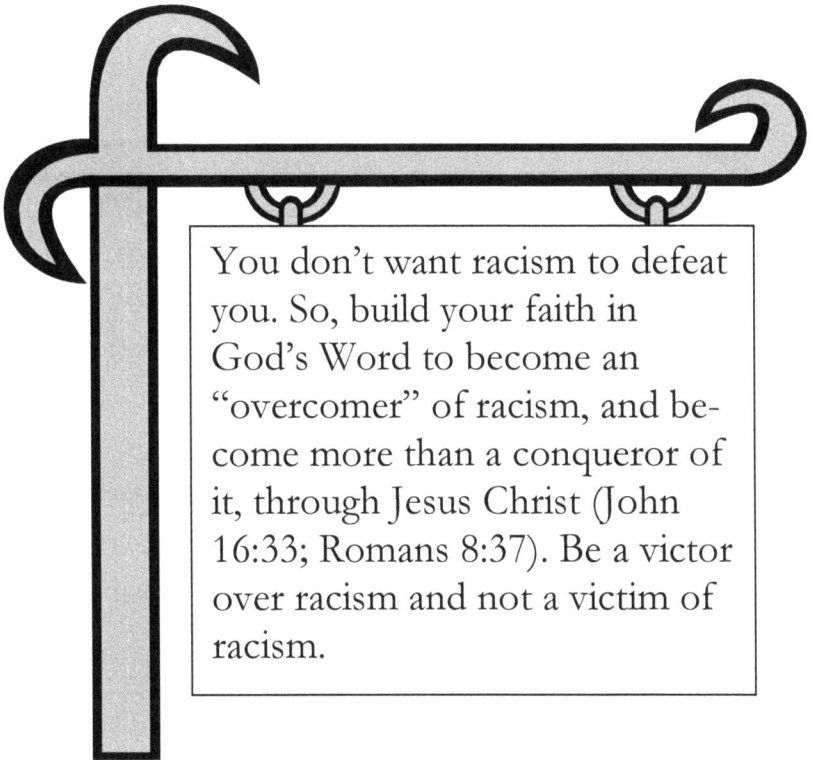

You don't want racism to defeat you. So, build your faith in God's Word to become an "overcomer" of racism, and become more than a conqueror of it, through Jesus Christ (John 16:33; Romans 8:37). Be a victor over racism and not a victim of racism.

18

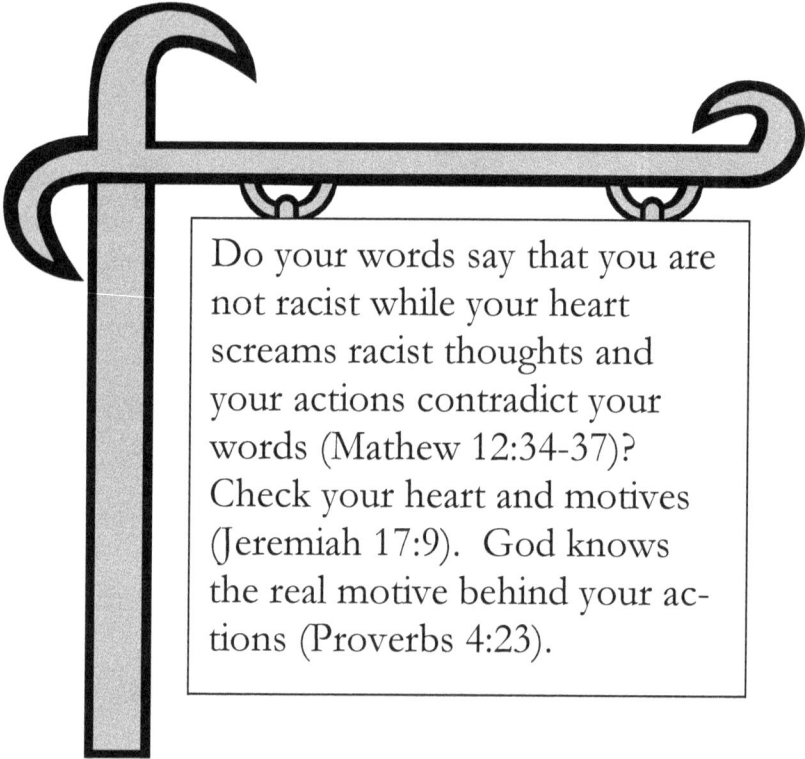

Do your words say that you are not racist while your heart screams racist thoughts and your actions contradict your words (Mathew 12:34-37)? Check your heart and motives (Jeremiah 17:9). God knows the real motive behind your actions (Proverbs 4:23).

19

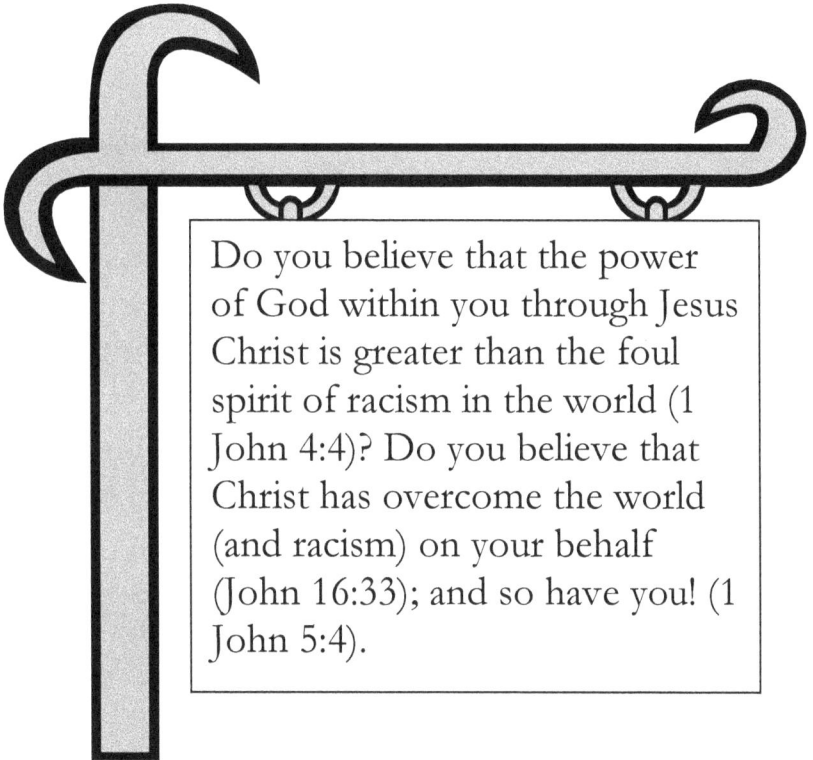

Do you believe that the power of God within you through Jesus Christ is greater than the foul spirit of racism in the world (1 John 4:4)? Do you believe that Christ has overcome the world (and racism) on your behalf (John 16:33); and so have you! (1 John 5:4).

20

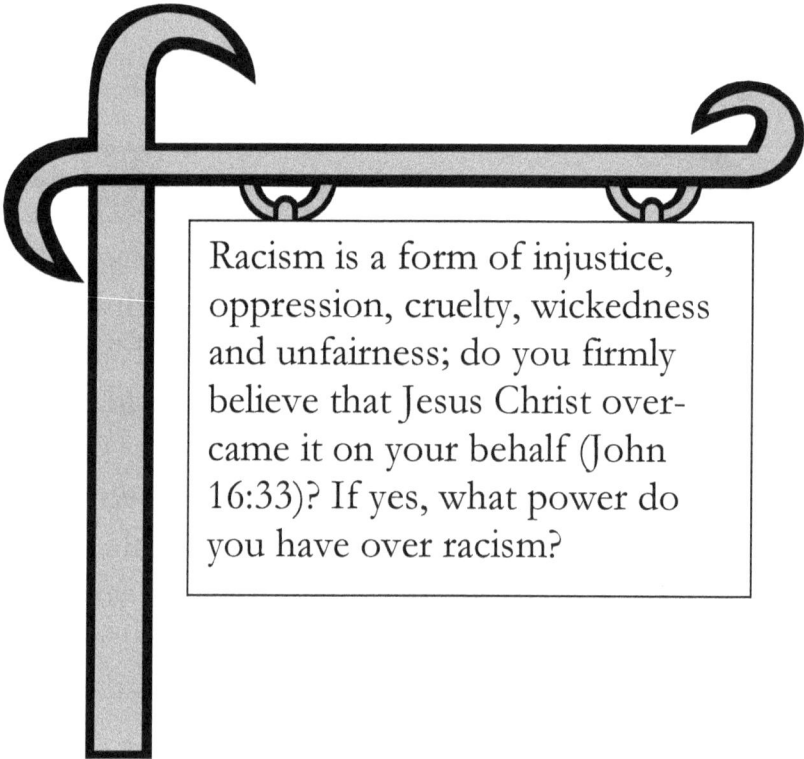

Racism is a form of injustice, oppression, cruelty, wickedness and unfairness; do you firmly believe that Jesus Christ over-came it on your behalf (John 16:33)? If yes, what power do you have over racism?

21

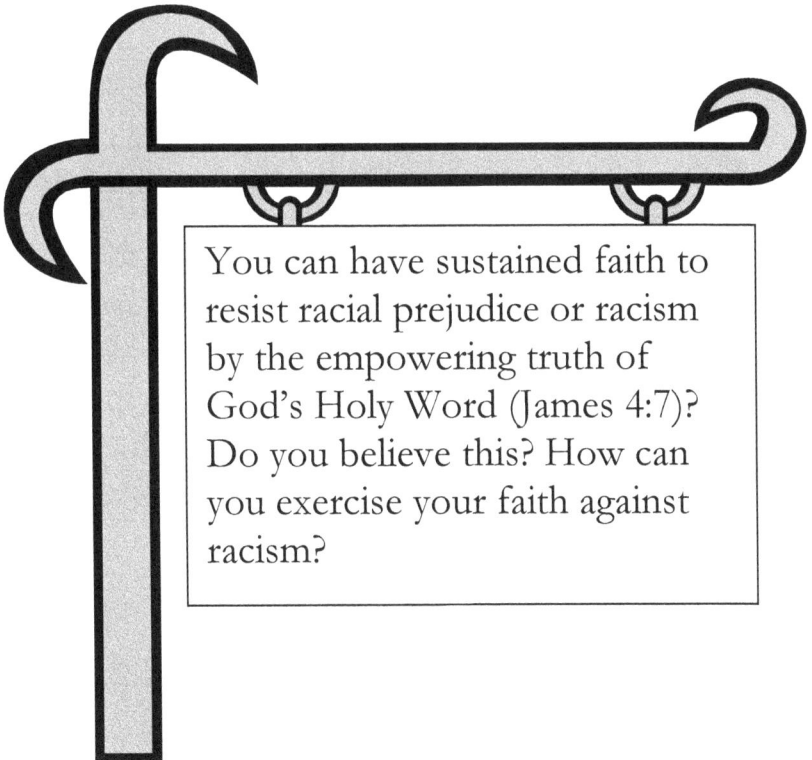

You can have sustained faith to resist racial prejudice or racism by the empowering truth of God's Holy Word (James 4:7)? Do you believe this? How can you exercise your faith against racism?

22

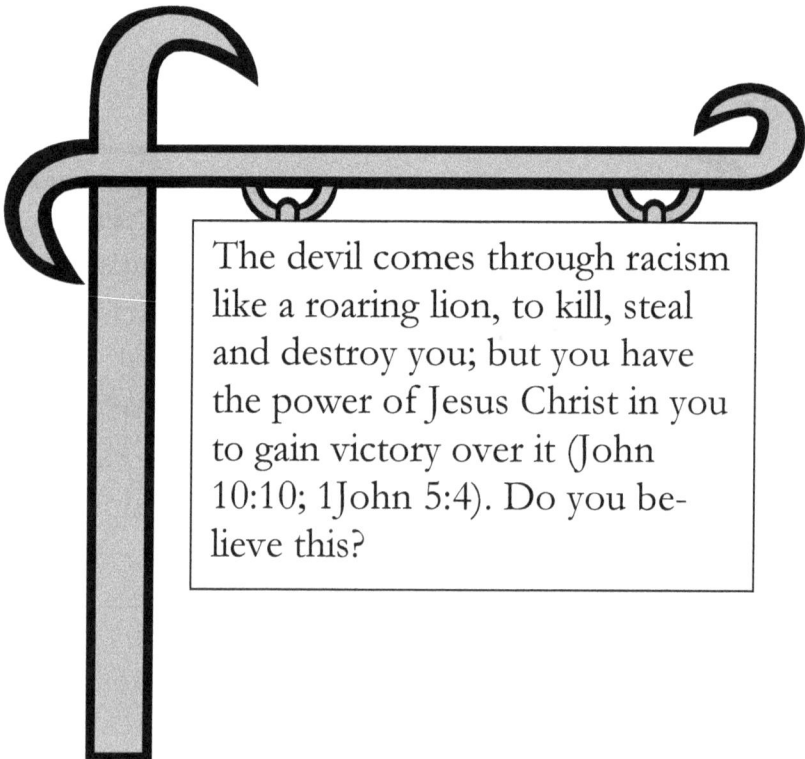

The devil comes through racism like a roaring lion, to kill, steal and destroy you; but you have the power of Jesus Christ in you to gain victory over it (John 10:10; 1John 5:4). Do you believe this?

23

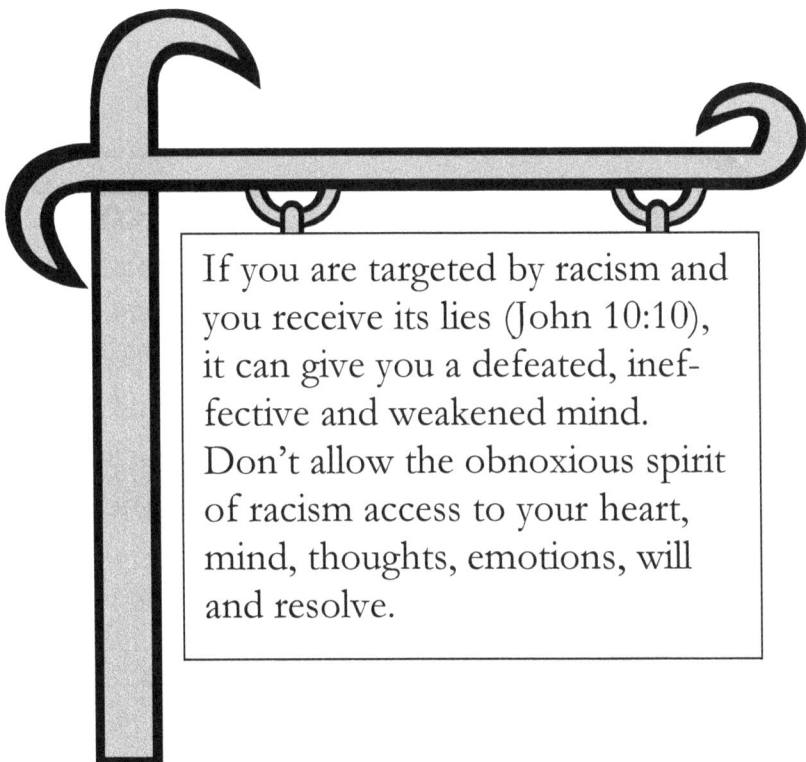

If you are targeted by racism and you receive its lies (John 10:10), it can give you a defeated, ineffective and weakened mind. Don't allow the obnoxious spirit of racism access to your heart, mind, thoughts, emotions, will and resolve.

24

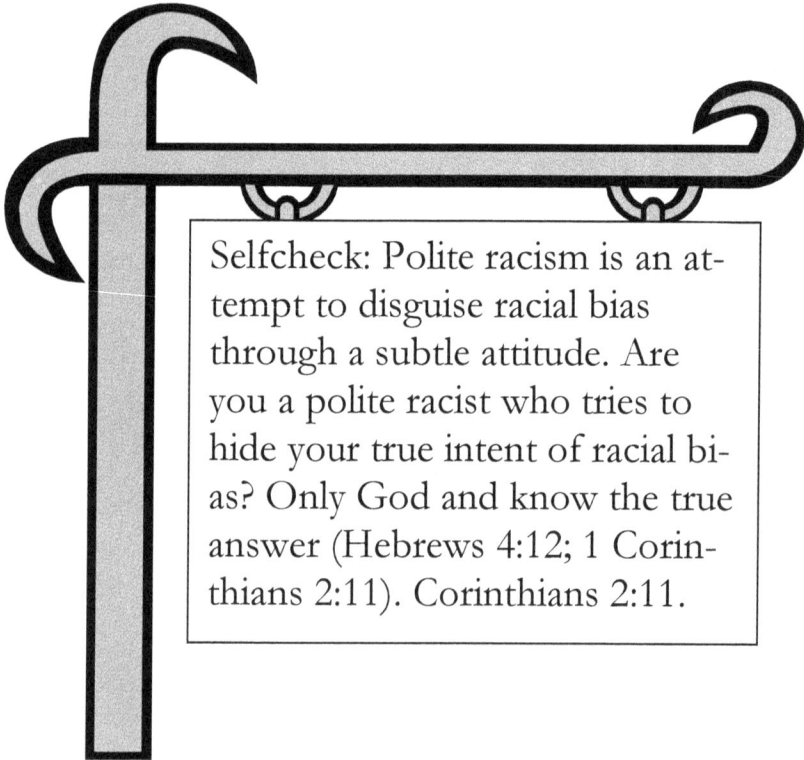

Selfcheck: Polite racism is an attempt to disguise racial bias through a subtle attitude. Are you a polite racist who tries to hide your true intent of racial bias? Only God and know the true answer (Hebrews 4:12; 1 Corinthians 2:11). Corinthians 2:11.

25

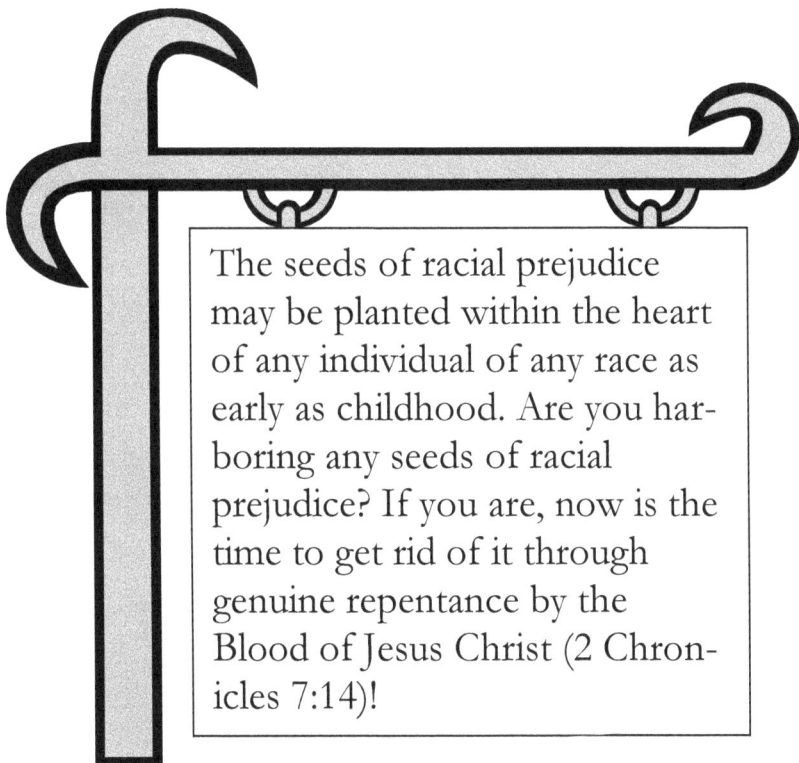

The seeds of racial prejudice may be planted within the heart of any individual of any race as early as childhood. Are you harboring any seeds of racial prejudice? If you are, now is the time to get rid of it through genuine repentance by the Blood of Jesus Christ (2 Chronicles 7:14)!

26

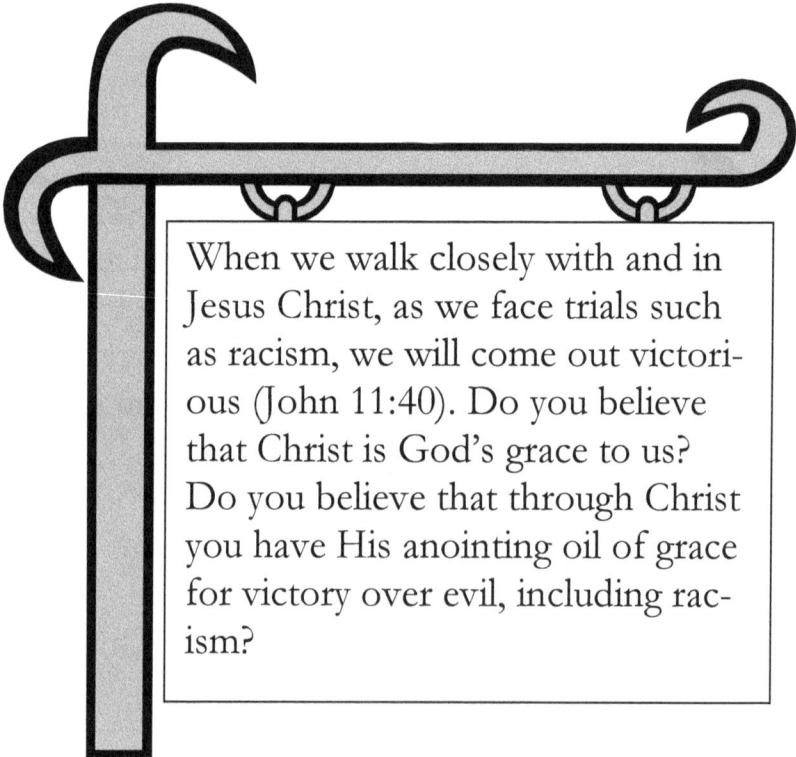

When we walk closely with and in Jesus Christ, as we face trials such as racism, we will come out victorious (John 11:40). Do you believe that Christ is God's grace to us? Do you believe that through Christ you have His anointing oil of grace for victory over evil, including racism?

27

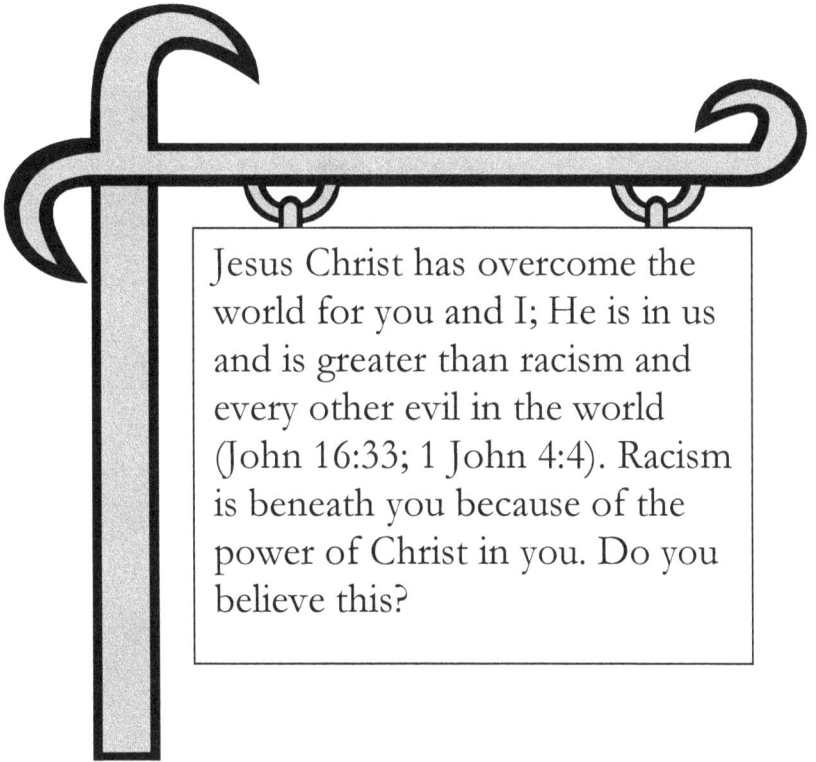

Jesus Christ has overcome the world for you and I; He is in us and is greater than racism and every other evil in the world (John 16:33; 1 John 4:4). Racism is beneath you because of the power of Christ in you. Do you believe this?

28

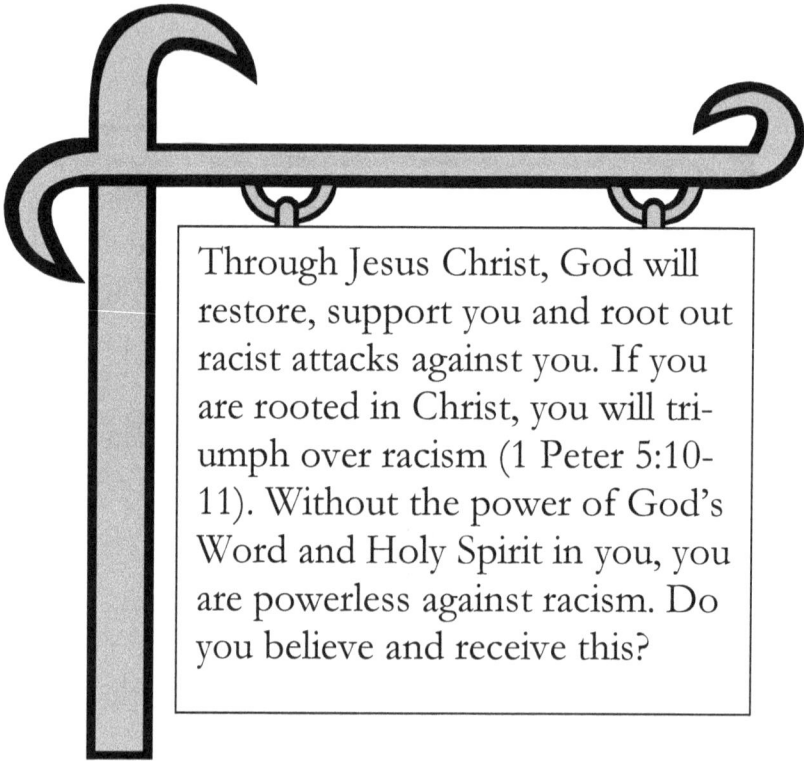

Through Jesus Christ, God will restore, support you and root out racist attacks against you. If you are rooted in Christ, you will triumph over racism (1 Peter 5:10-11). Without the power of God's Word and Holy Spirit in you, you are powerless against racism. Do you believe and receive this?

29

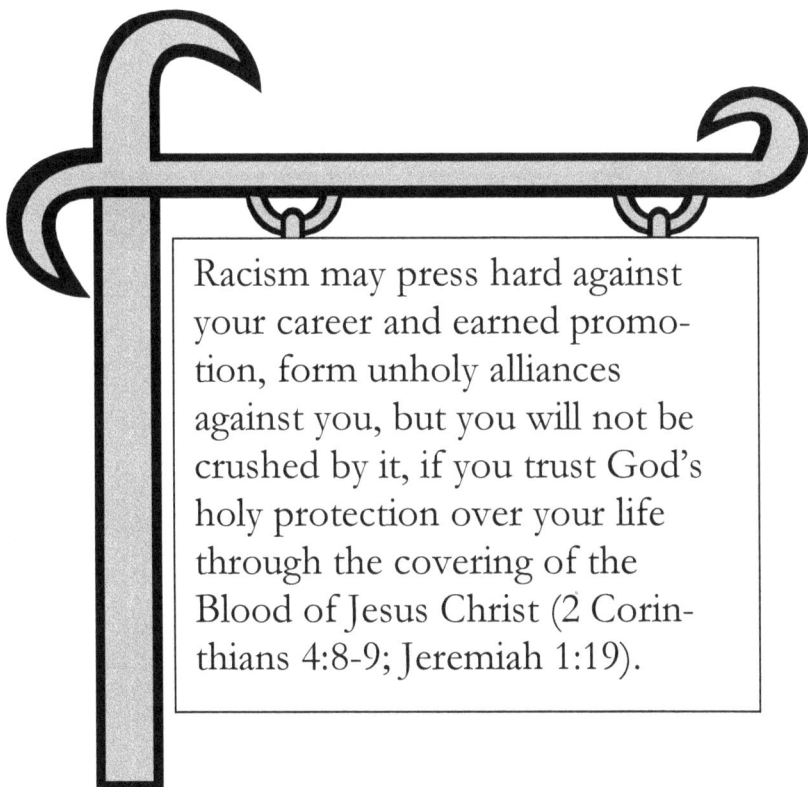

Racism may press hard against your career and earned promotion, form unholy alliances against you, but you will not be crushed by it, if you trust God's holy protection over your life through the covering of the Blood of Jesus Christ (2 Corinthians 4:8-9; Jeremiah 1:19).

30

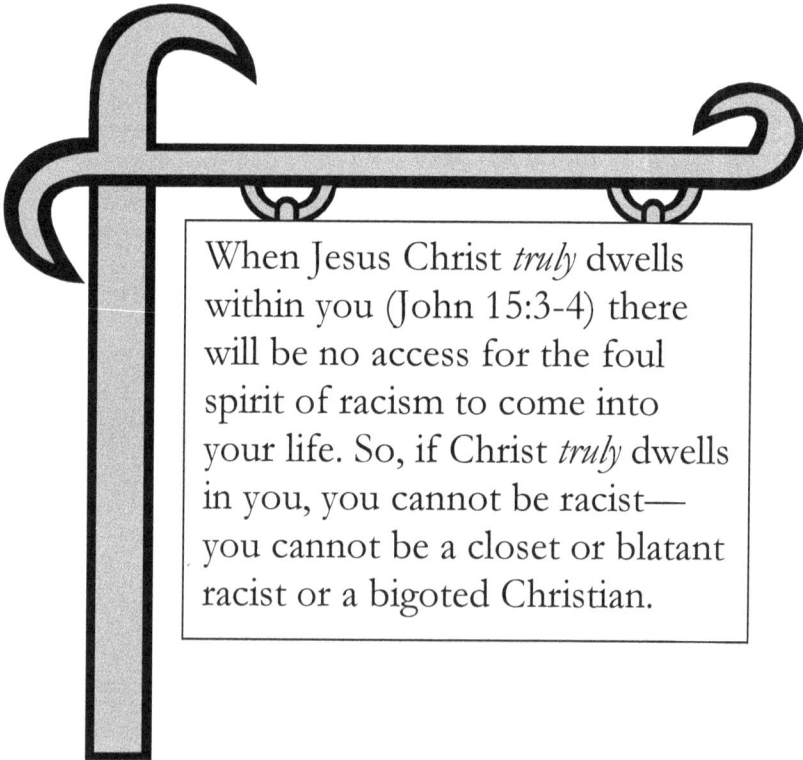

When Jesus Christ *truly* dwells within you (John 15:3-4) there will be no access for the foul spirit of racism to come into your life. So, if Christ *truly* dwells in you, you cannot be racist—you cannot be a closet or blatant racist or a bigoted Christian.

31

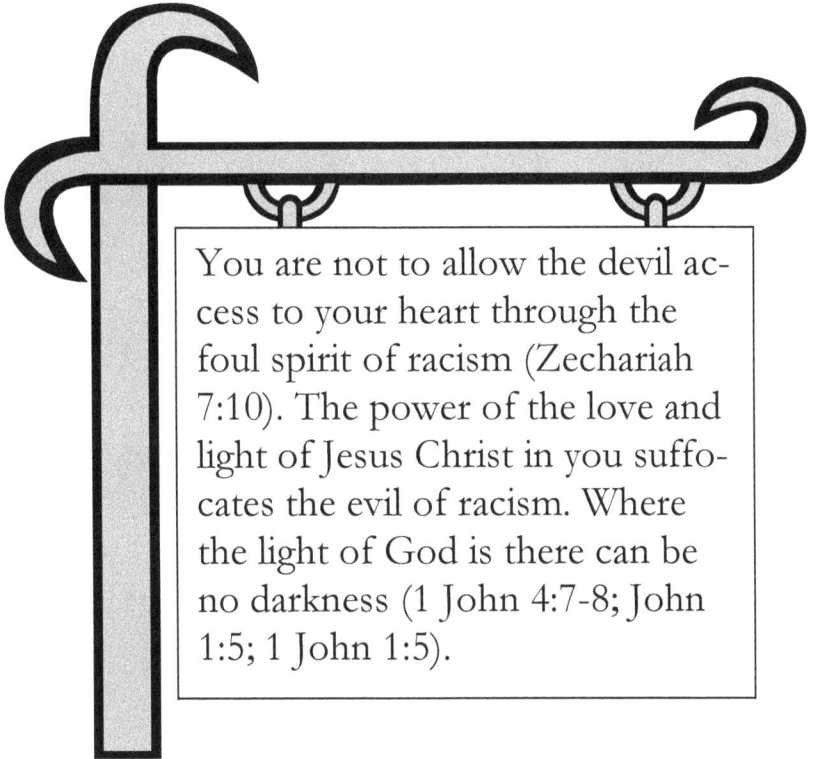

You are not to allow the devil access to your heart through the foul spirit of racism (Zechariah 7:10). The power of the love and light of Jesus Christ in you suffocates the evil of racism. Where the light of God is there can be no darkness (1 John 4:7-8; John 1:5; 1 John 1:5).

32

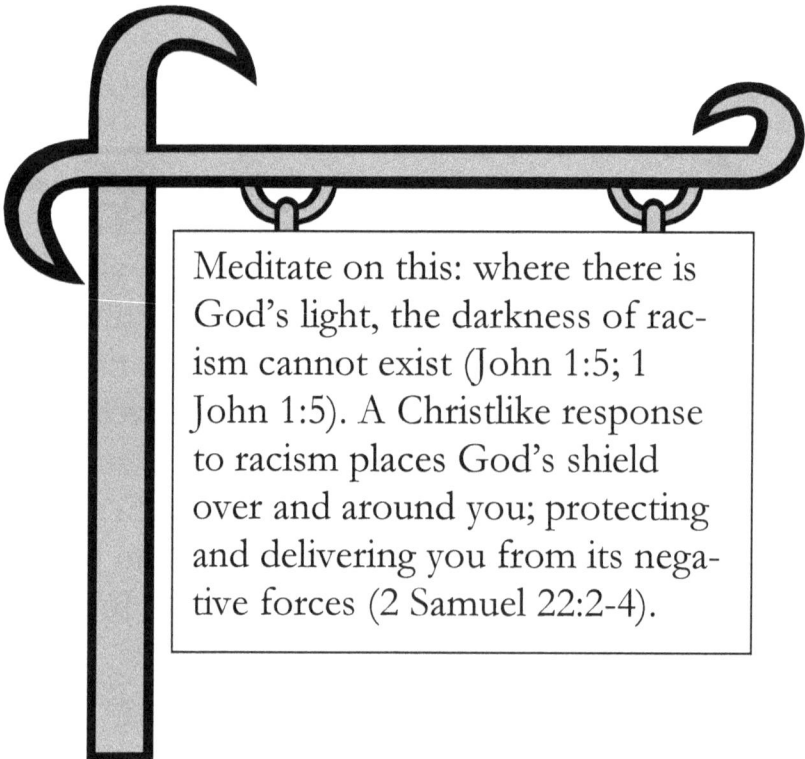

Meditate on this: where there is God's light, the darkness of racism cannot exist (John 1:5; 1 John 1:5). A Christlike response to racism places God's shield over and around you; protecting and delivering you from its negative forces (2 Samuel 22:2-4).

33

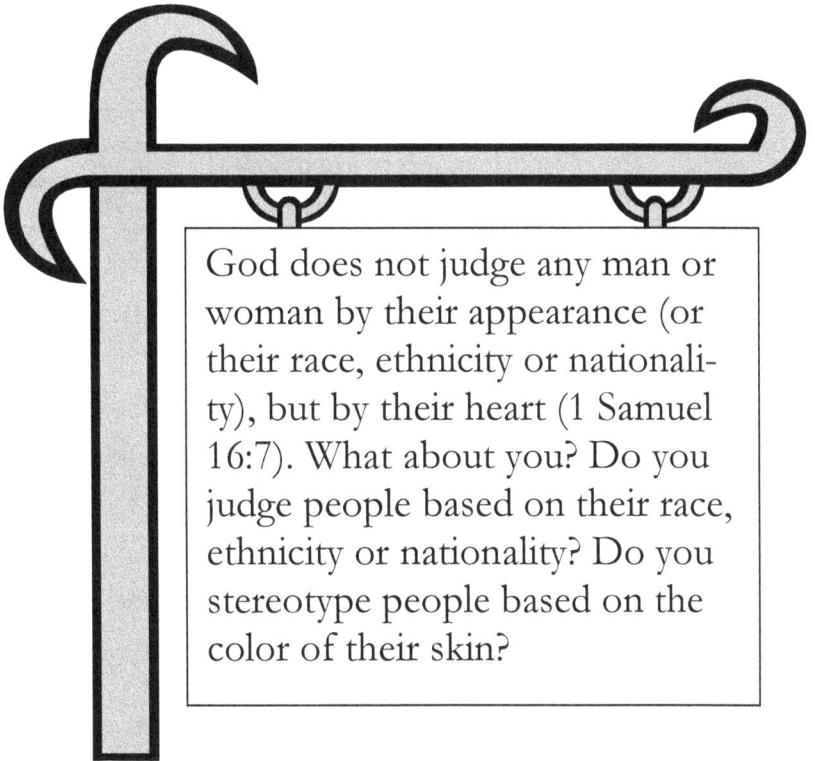

God does not judge any man or woman by their appearance (or their race, ethnicity or nationality), but by their heart (1 Samuel 16:7). What about you? Do you judge people based on their race, ethnicity or nationality? Do you stereotype people based on the color of their skin?

34

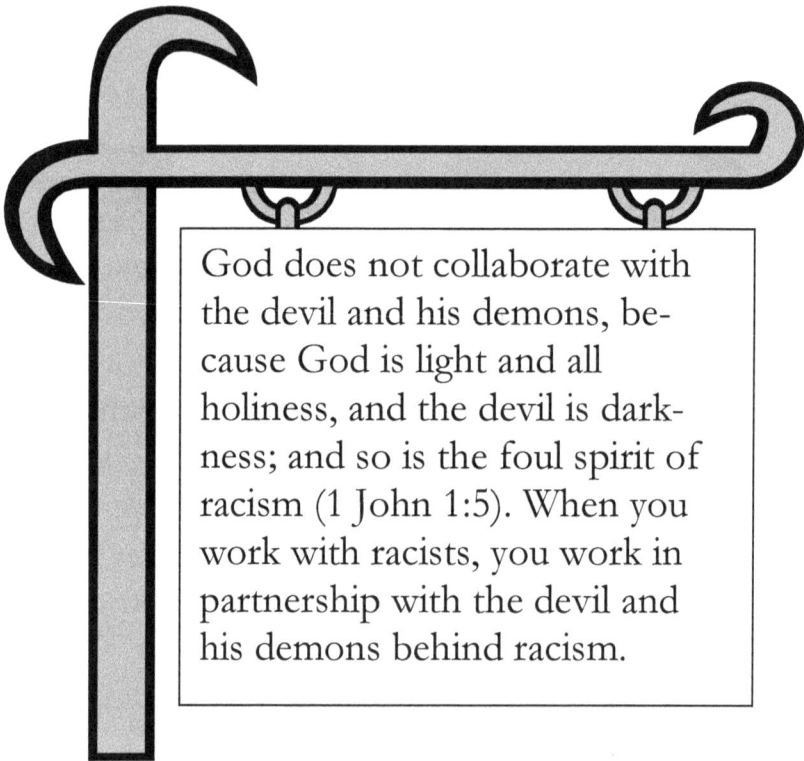

God does not collaborate with the devil and his demons, because God is light and all holiness, and the devil is darkness; and so is the foul spirit of racism (1 John 1:5). When you work with racists, you work in partnership with the devil and his demons behind racism.

35

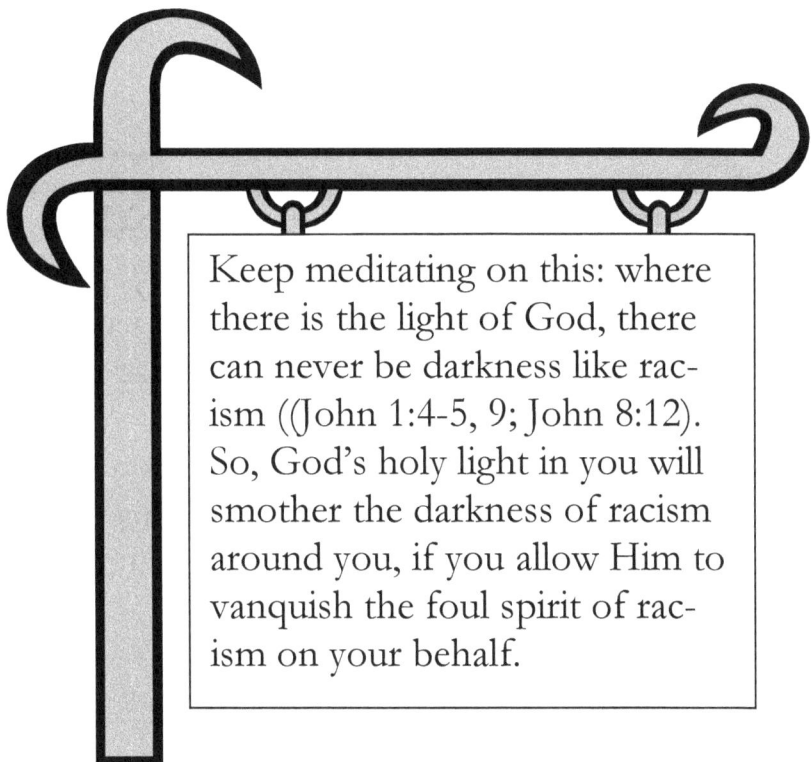

Keep meditating on this: where there is the light of God, there can never be darkness like racism ((John 1:4-5, 9; John 8:12). So, God's holy light in you will smother the darkness of racism around you, if you allow Him to vanquish the foul spirit of racism on your behalf.

36

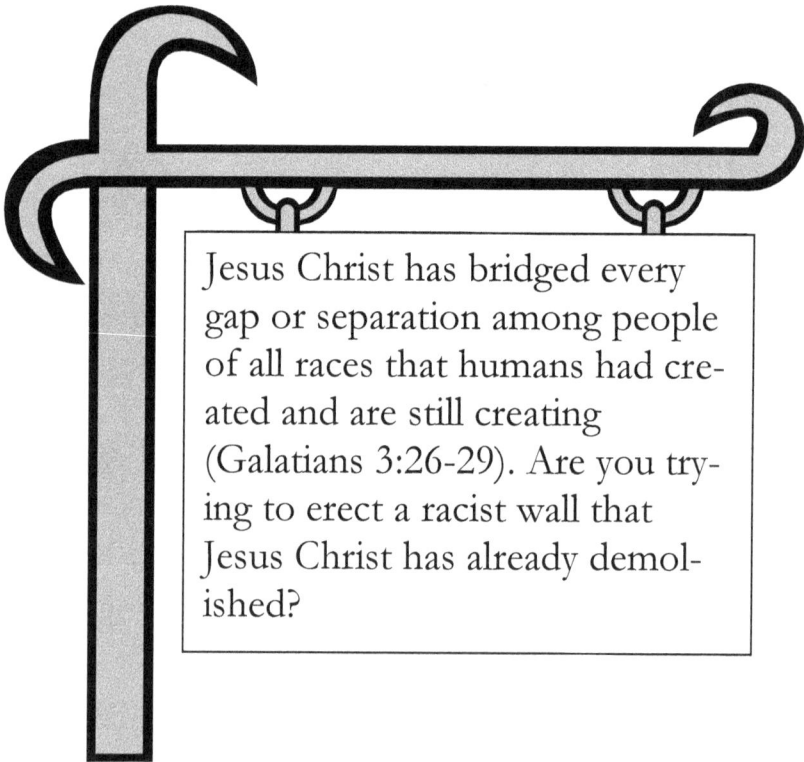

Jesus Christ has bridged every gap or separation among people of all races that humans had created and are still creating (Galatians 3:26-29). Are you trying to erect a racist wall that Jesus Christ has already demolished?

37

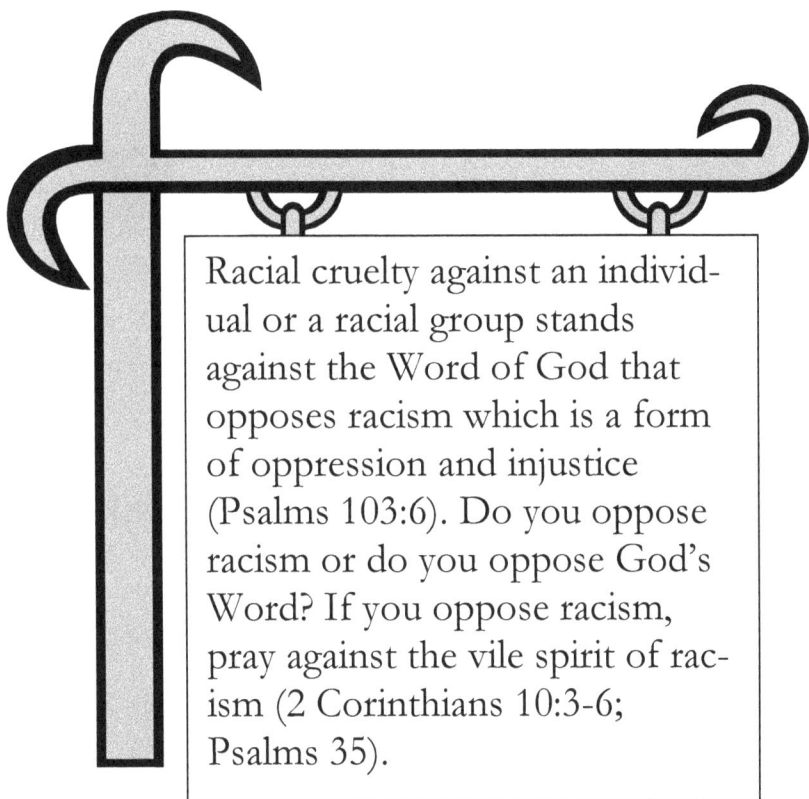

Racial cruelty against an individual or a racial group stands against the Word of God that opposes racism which is a form of oppression and injustice (Psalms 103:6). Do you oppose racism or do you oppose God's Word? If you oppose racism, pray against the vile spirit of racism (2 Corinthians 10:3-6; Psalms 35).

38

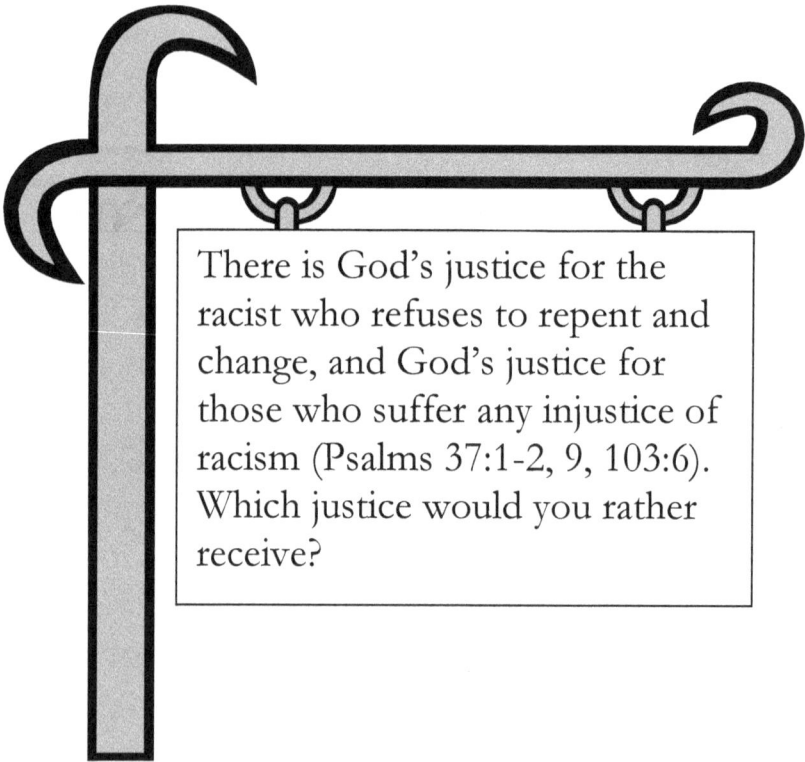

There is God's justice for the racist who refuses to repent and change, and God's justice for those who suffer any injustice of racism (Psalms 37:1-2, 9, 103:6). Which justice would you rather receive?

39

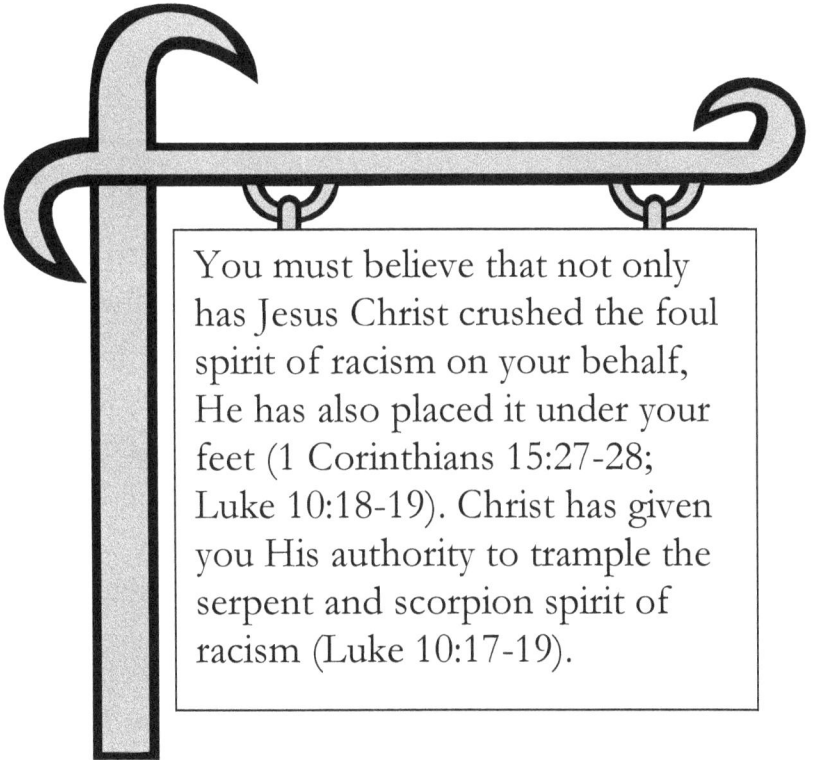

You must believe that not only has Jesus Christ crushed the foul spirit of racism on your behalf, He has also placed it under your feet (1 Corinthians 15:27-28; Luke 10:18-19). Christ has given you His authority to trample the serpent and scorpion spirit of racism (Luke 10:17-19).

40

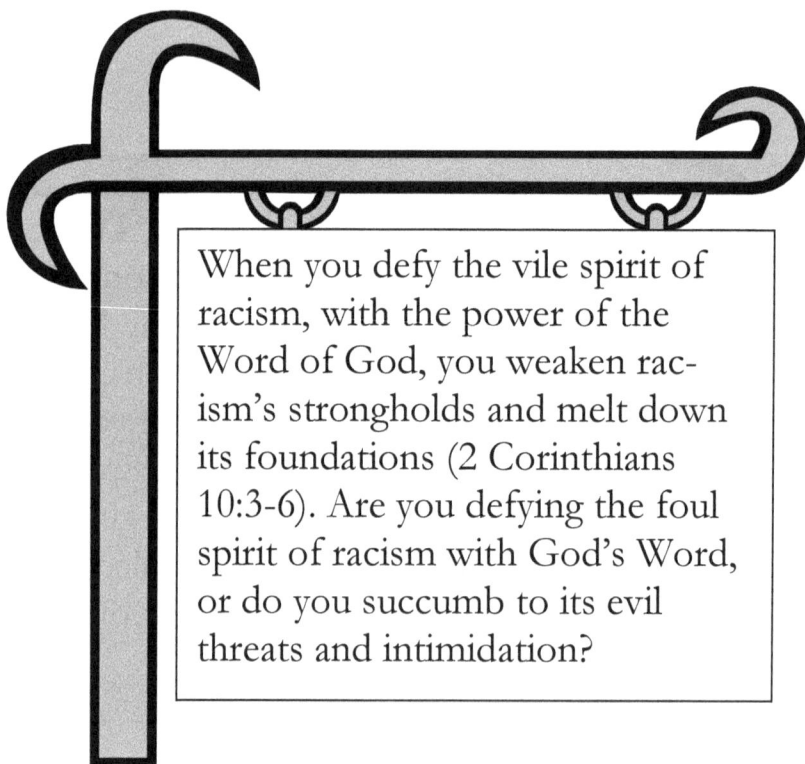

When you defy the vile spirit of racism, with the power of the Word of God, you weaken racism's strongholds and melt down its foundations (2 Corinthians 10:3-6). Are you defying the foul spirit of racism with God's Word, or do you succumb to its evil threats and intimidation?

41

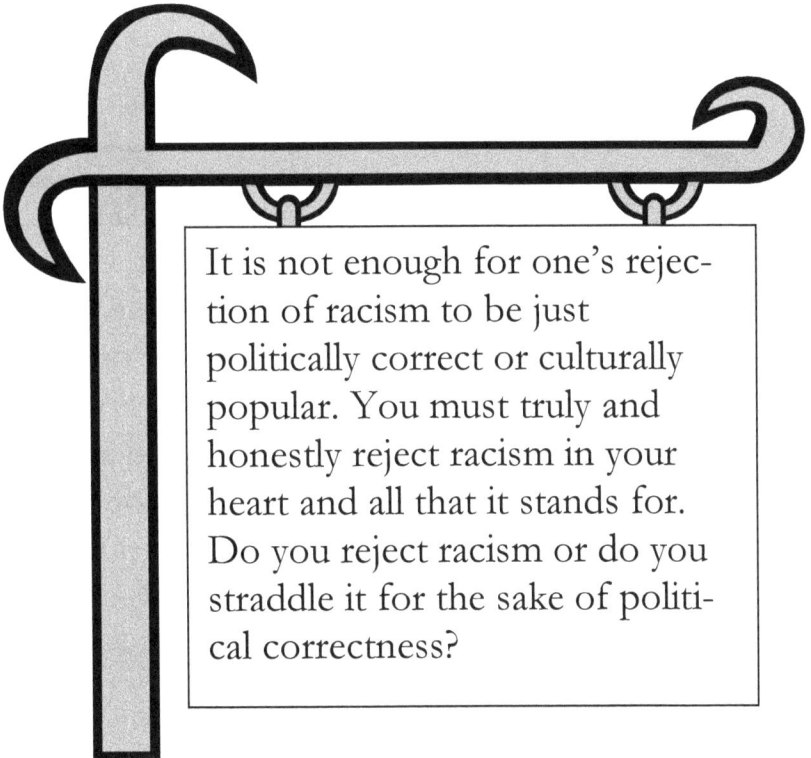

It is not enough for one's rejection of racism to be just politically correct or culturally popular. You must truly and honestly reject racism in your heart and all that it stands for. Do you reject racism or do you straddle it for the sake of political correctness?

42

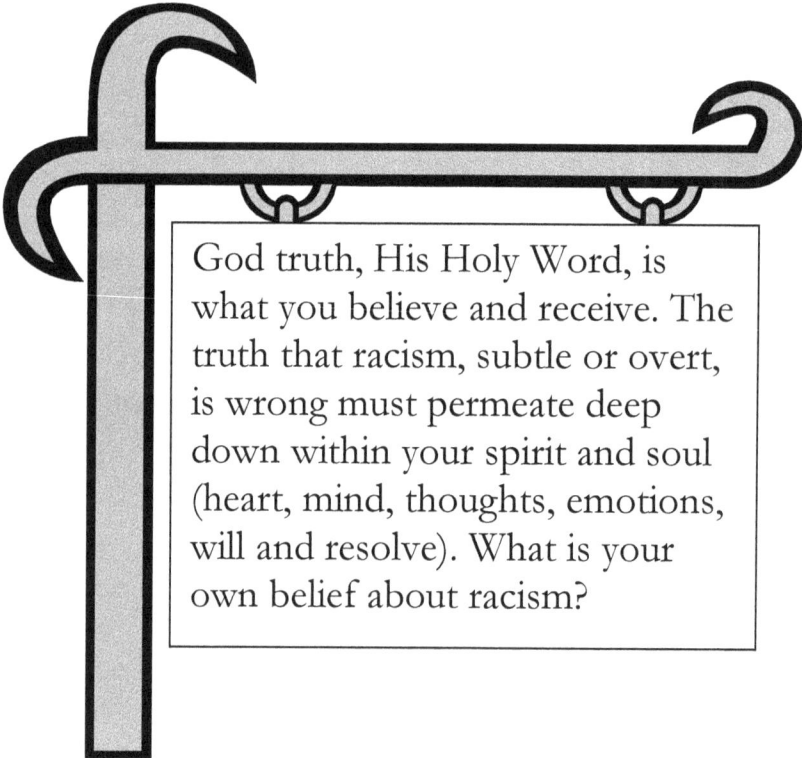

God truth, His Holy Word, is what you believe and receive. The truth that racism, subtle or overt, is wrong must permeate deep down within your spirit and soul (heart, mind, thoughts, emotions, will and resolve). What is your own belief about racism?

43

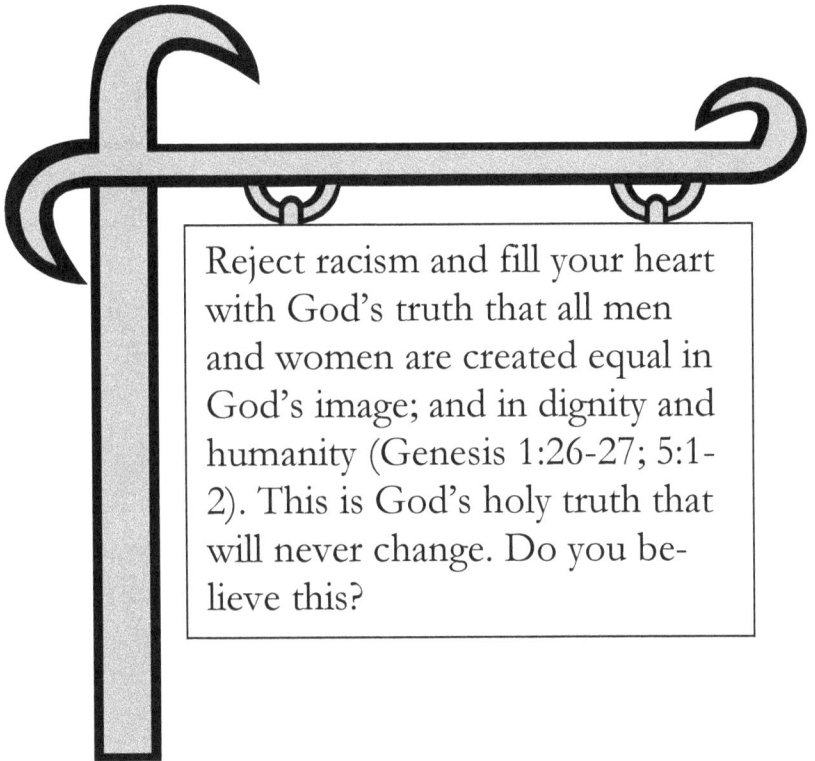

Reject racism and fill your heart with God's truth that all men and women are created equal in God's image; and in dignity and humanity (Genesis 1:26-27; 5:1-2). This is God's holy truth that will never change. Do you believe this?

44

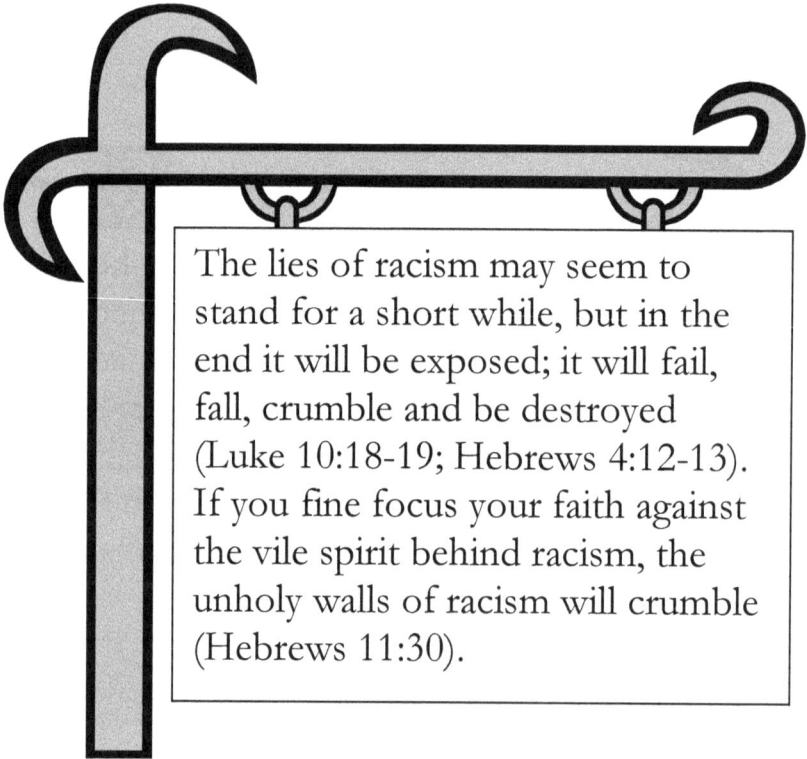

The lies of racism may seem to stand for a short while, but in the end it will be exposed; it will fail, fall, crumble and be destroyed (Luke 10:18-19; Hebrews 4:12-13). If you fine focus your faith against the vile spirit behind racism, the unholy walls of racism will crumble (Hebrews 11:30).

45

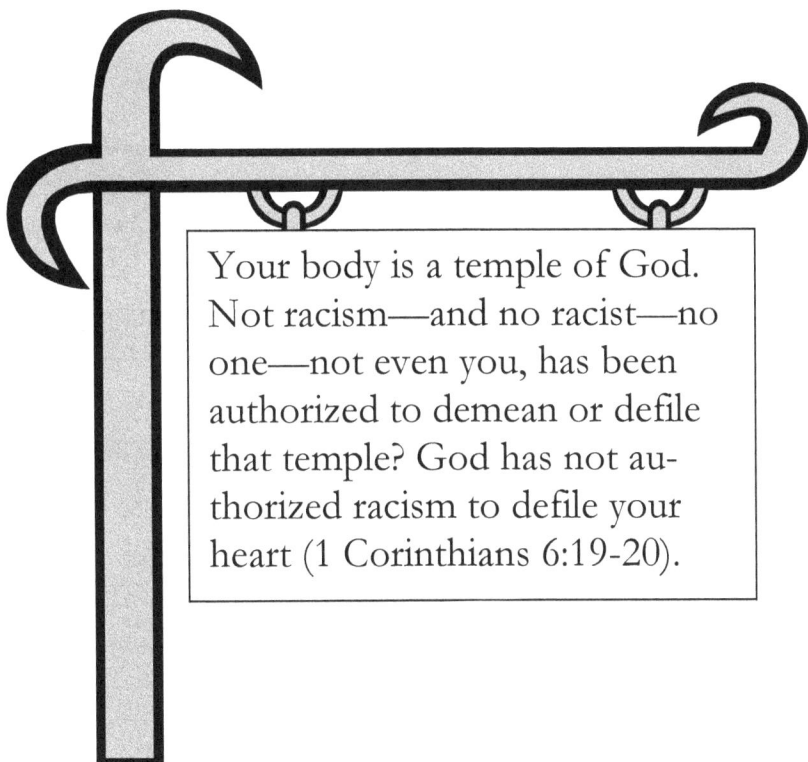

Your body is a temple of God. Not racism—and no racist—no one—not even you, has been authorized to demean or defile that temple? God has not authorized racism to defile your heart (1 Corinthians 6:19-20).

46

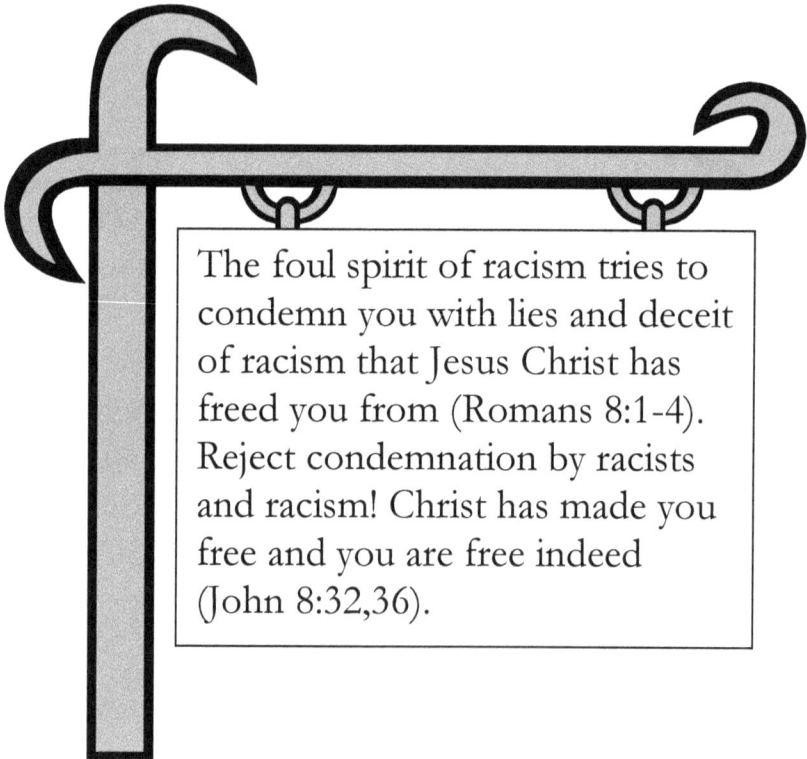

The foul spirit of racism tries to condemn you with lies and deceit of racism that Jesus Christ has freed you from (Romans 8:1-4). Reject condemnation by racists and racism! Christ has made you free and you are free indeed (John 8:32,36).

47

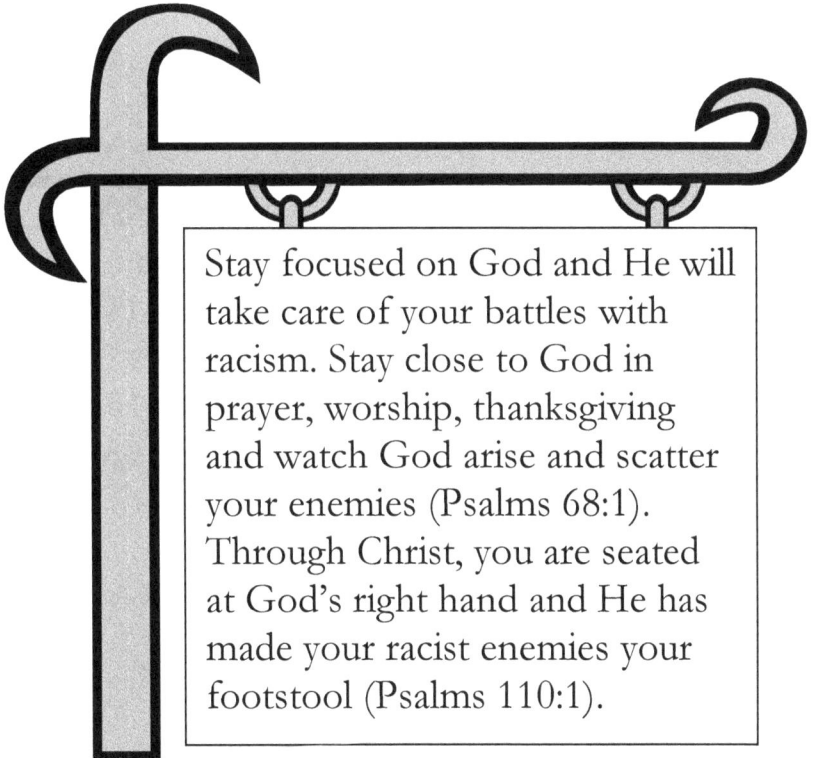

Stay focused on God and He will take care of your battles with racism. Stay close to God in prayer, worship, thanksgiving and watch God arise and scatter your enemies (Psalms 68:1). Through Christ, you are seated at God's right hand and He has made your racist enemies your footstool (Psalms 110:1).

48

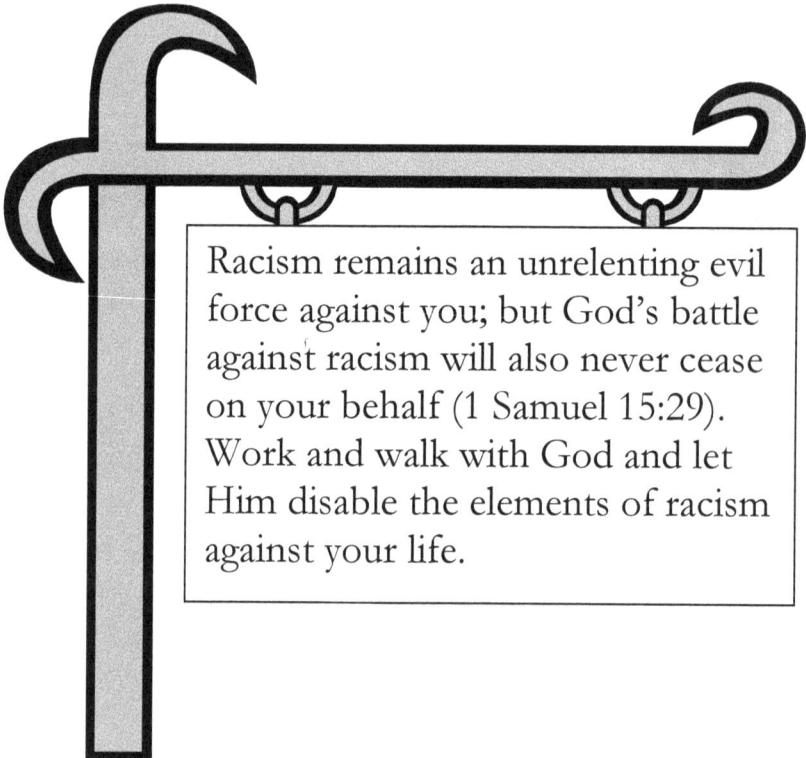

Racism remains an unrelenting evil force against you; but God's battle against racism will also never cease on your behalf (1 Samuel 15:29). Work and walk with God and let Him disable the elements of racism against your life.

49

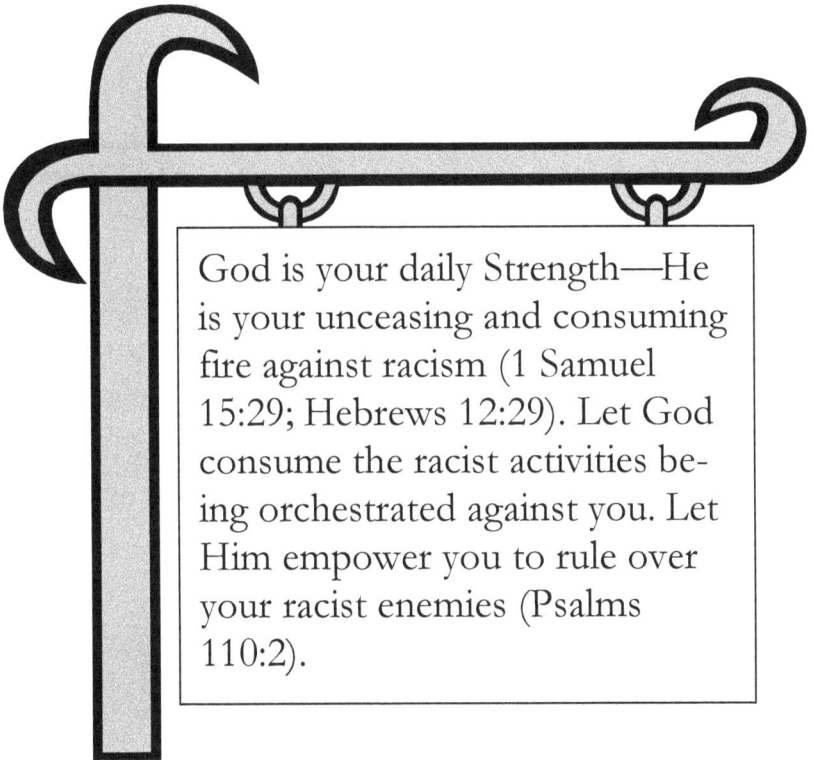

God is your daily Strength—He is your unceasing and consuming fire against racism (1 Samuel 15:29; Hebrews 12:29). Let God consume the racist activities being orchestrated against you. Let Him empower you to rule over your racist enemies (Psalms 110:2).

50

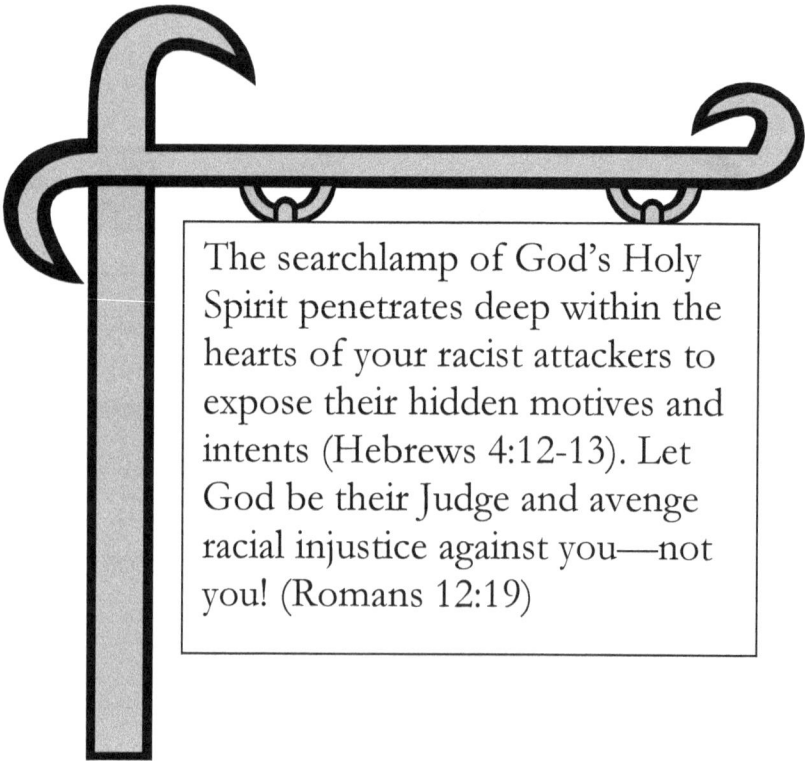

The searchlamp of God's Holy Spirit penetrates deep within the hearts of your racist attackers to expose their hidden motives and intents (Hebrews 4:12-13). Let God be their Judge and avenge racial injustice against you—not you! (Romans 12:19)

51

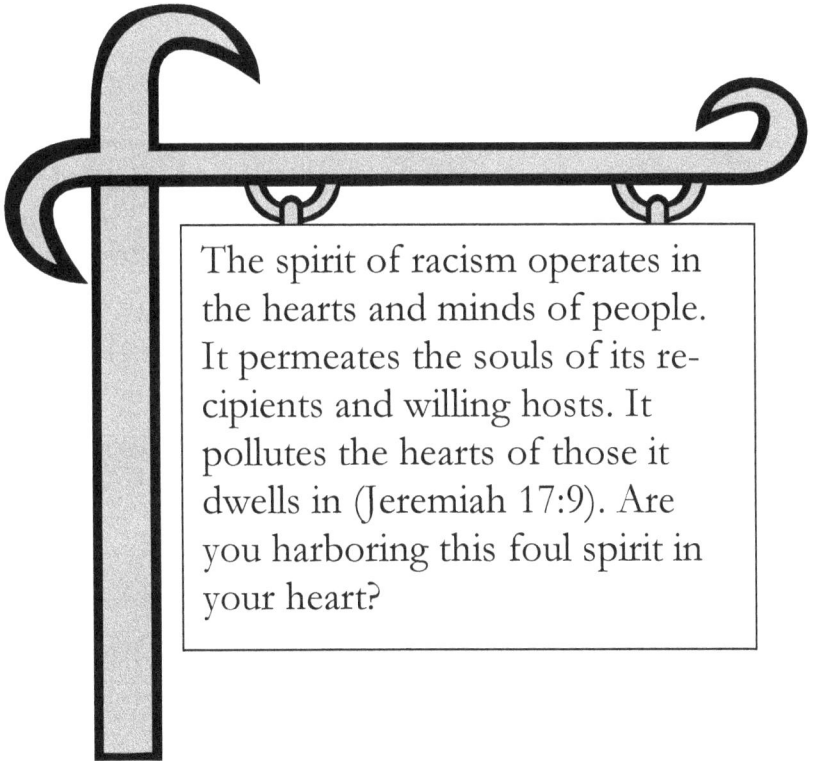

The spirit of racism operates in the hearts and minds of people. It permeates the souls of its recipients and willing hosts. It pollutes the hearts of those it dwells in (Jeremiah 17:9). Are you harboring this foul spirit in your heart?

52

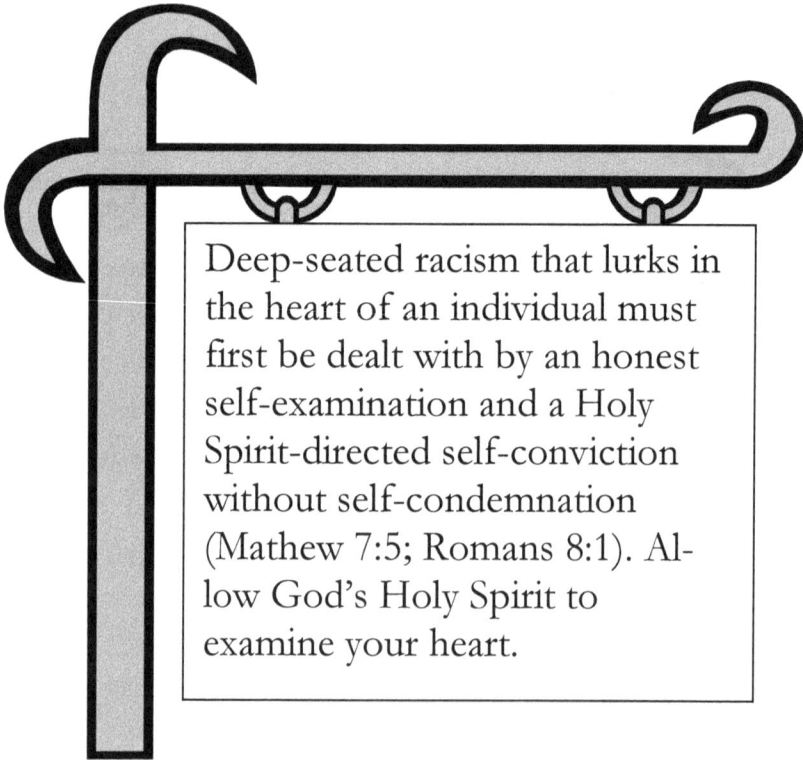

Deep-seated racism that lurks in the heart of an individual must first be dealt with by an honest self-examination and a Holy Spirit-directed self-conviction without self-condemnation (Mathew 7:5; Romans 8:1). Allow God's Holy Spirit to examine your heart.

53

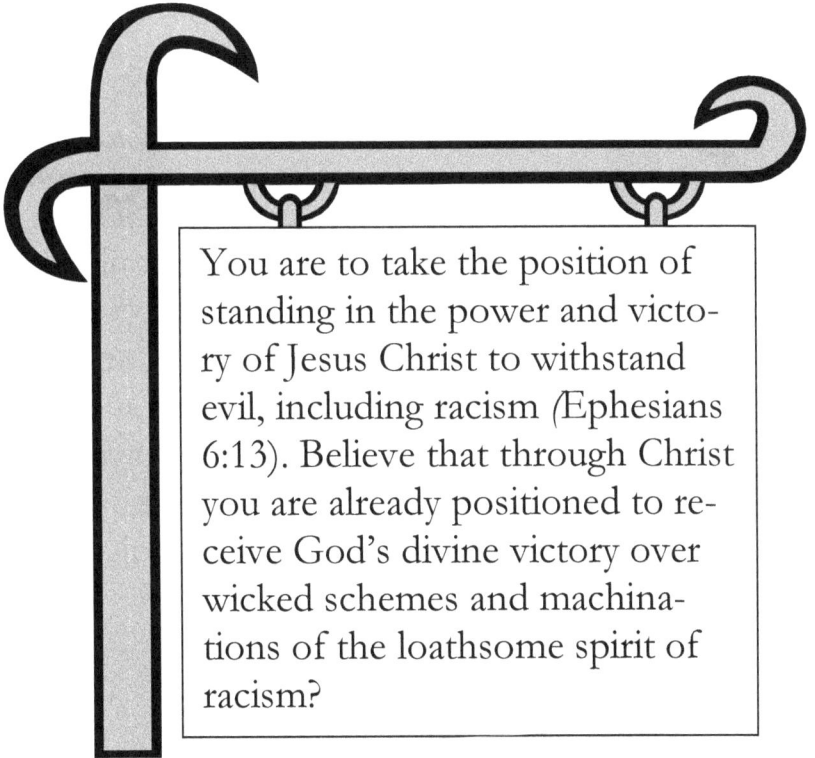

You are to take the position of standing in the power and victory of Jesus Christ to withstand evil, including racism (Ephesians 6:13). Believe that through Christ you are already positioned to receive God's divine victory over wicked schemes and machinations of the loathsome spirit of racism?

54

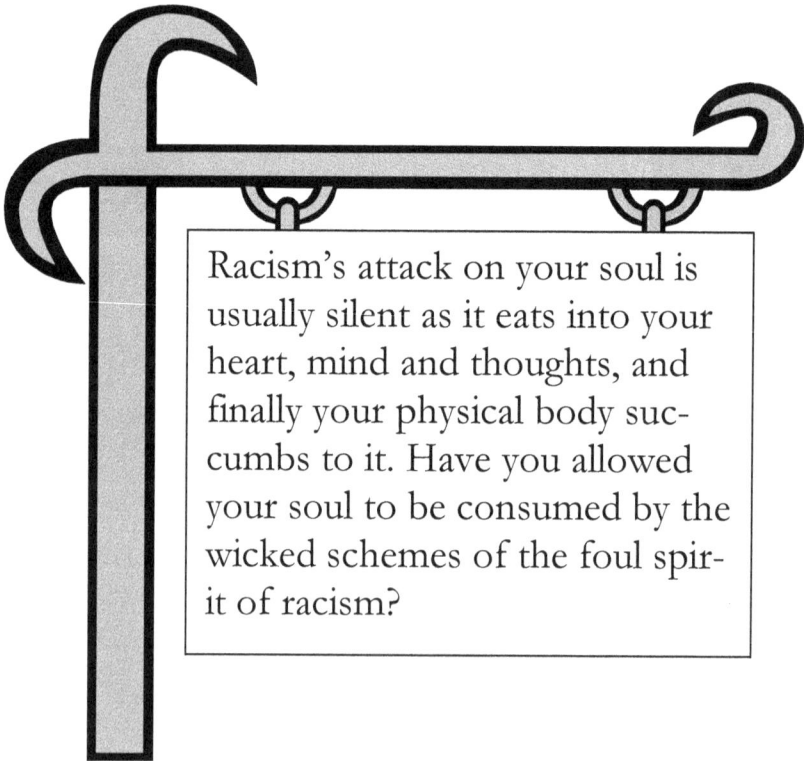

Racism's attack on your soul is usually silent as it eats into your heart, mind and thoughts, and finally your physical body succumbs to it. Have you allowed your soul to be consumed by the wicked schemes of the foul spirit of racism?

55

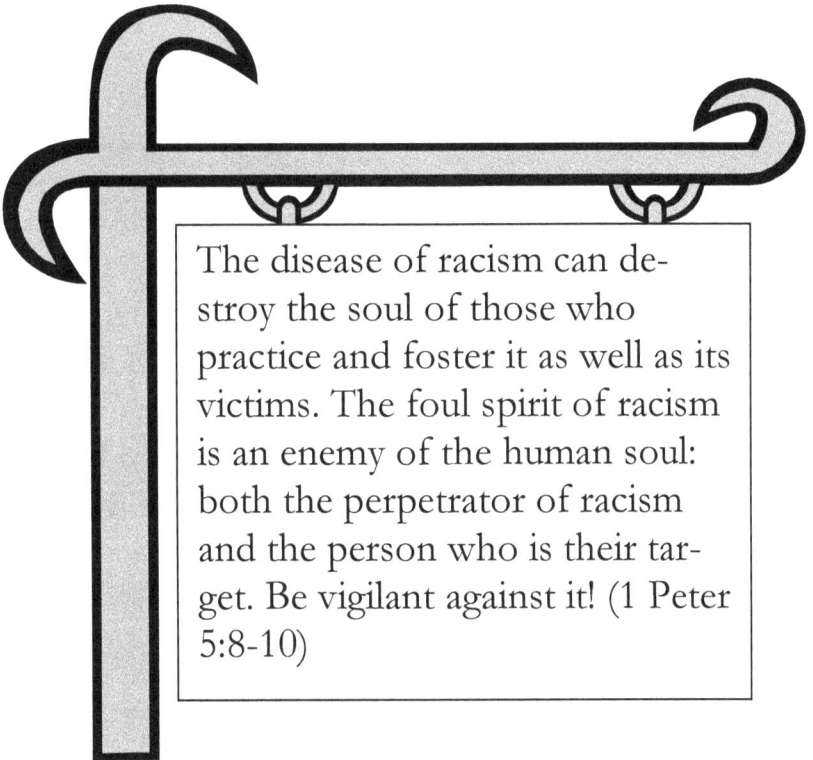

The disease of racism can destroy the soul of those who practice and foster it as well as its victims. The foul spirit of racism is an enemy of the human soul: both the perpetrator of racism and the person who is their target. Be vigilant against it! (1 Peter 5:8-10)

56

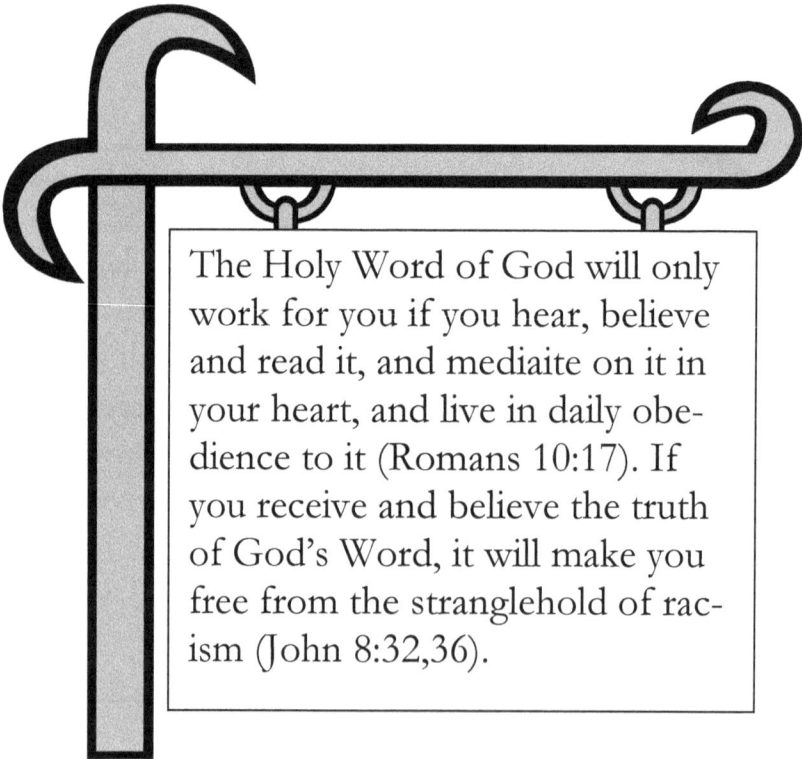

The Holy Word of God will only work for you if you hear, believe and read it, and mediaite on it in your heart, and live in daily obedience to it (Romans 10:17). If you receive and believe the truth of God's Word, it will make you free from the stranglehold of racism (John 8:32,36).

57

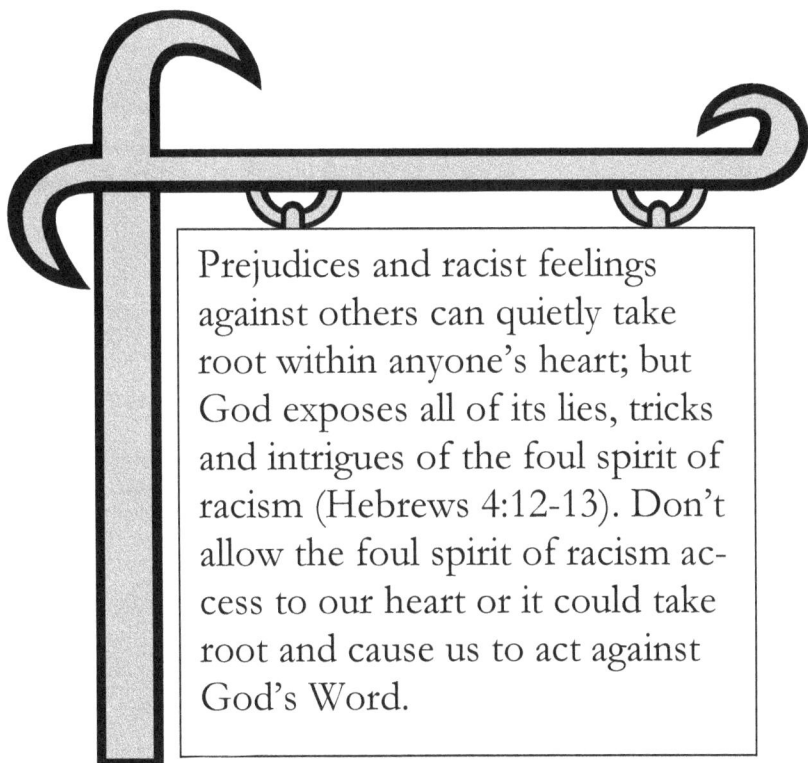

Prejudices and racist feelings against others can quietly take root within anyone's heart; but God exposes all of its lies, tricks and intrigues of the foul spirit of racism (Hebrews 4:12-13). Don't allow the foul spirit of racism access to our heart or it could take root and cause us to act against God's Word.

58

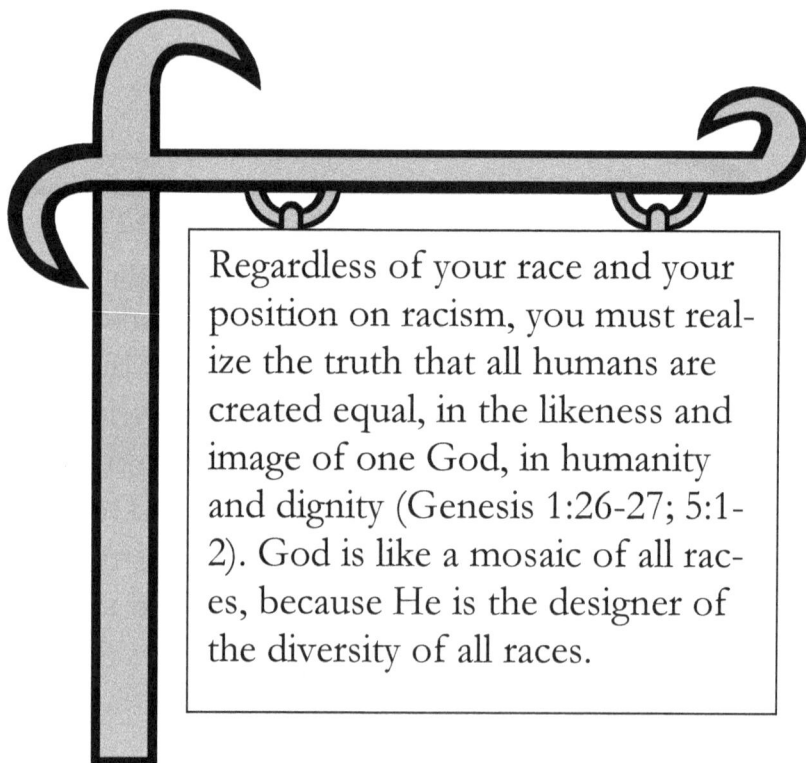

Regardless of your race and your position on racism, you must realize the truth that all humans are created equal, in the likeness and image of one God, in humanity and dignity (Genesis 1:26-27; 5:1-2). God is like a mosaic of all races, because He is the designer of the diversity of all races.

59

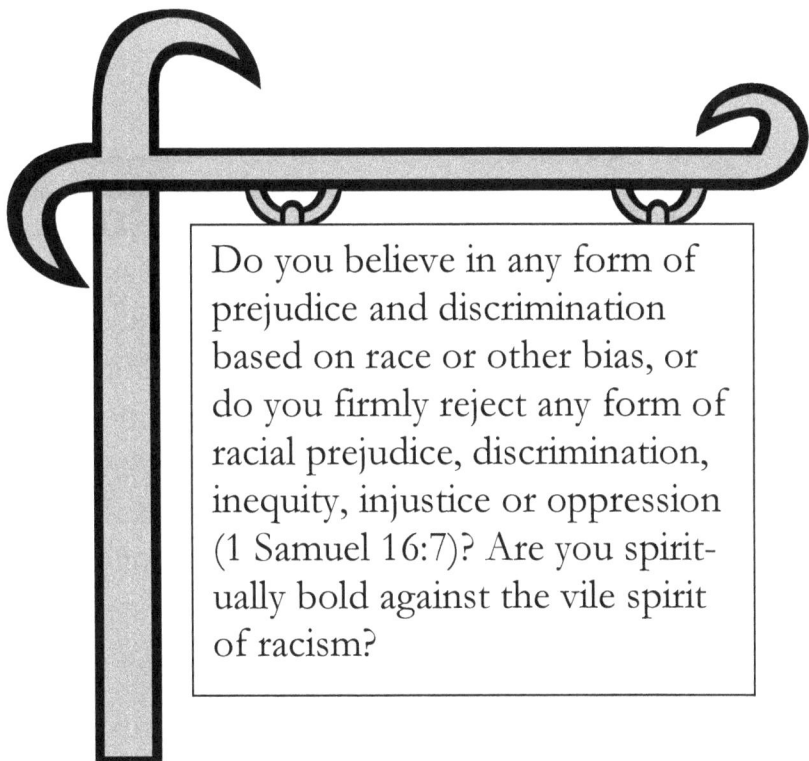

Do you believe in any form of prejudice and discrimination based on race or other bias, or do you firmly reject any form of racial prejudice, discrimination, inequity, injustice or oppression (1 Samuel 16:7)? Are you spiritually bold against the vile spirit of racism?

60

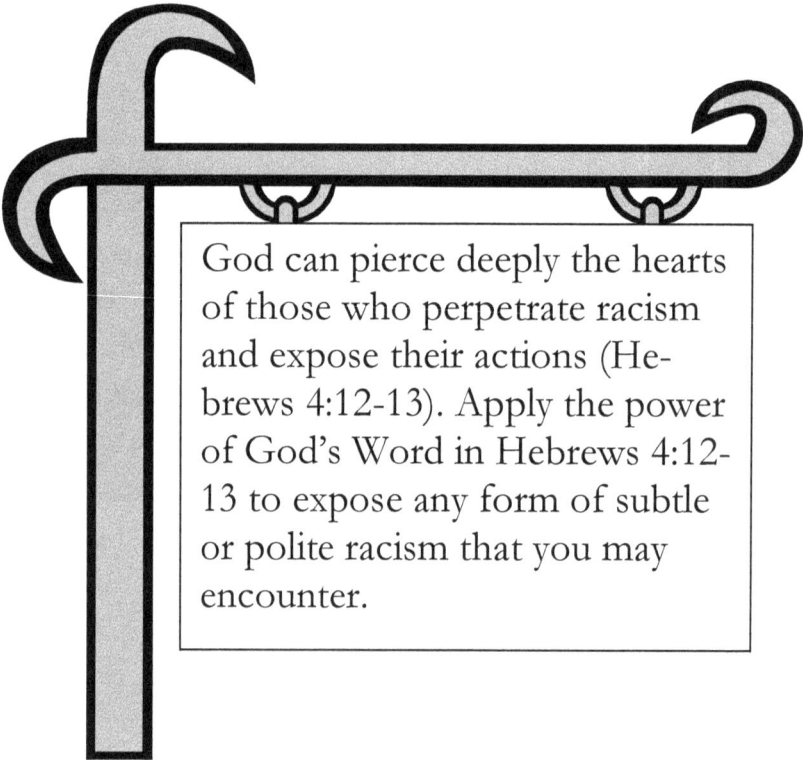

God can pierce deeply the hearts of those who perpetrate racism and expose their actions (Hebrews 4:12-13). Apply the power of God's Word in Hebrews 4:12-13 to expose any form of subtle or polite racism that you may encounter.

61

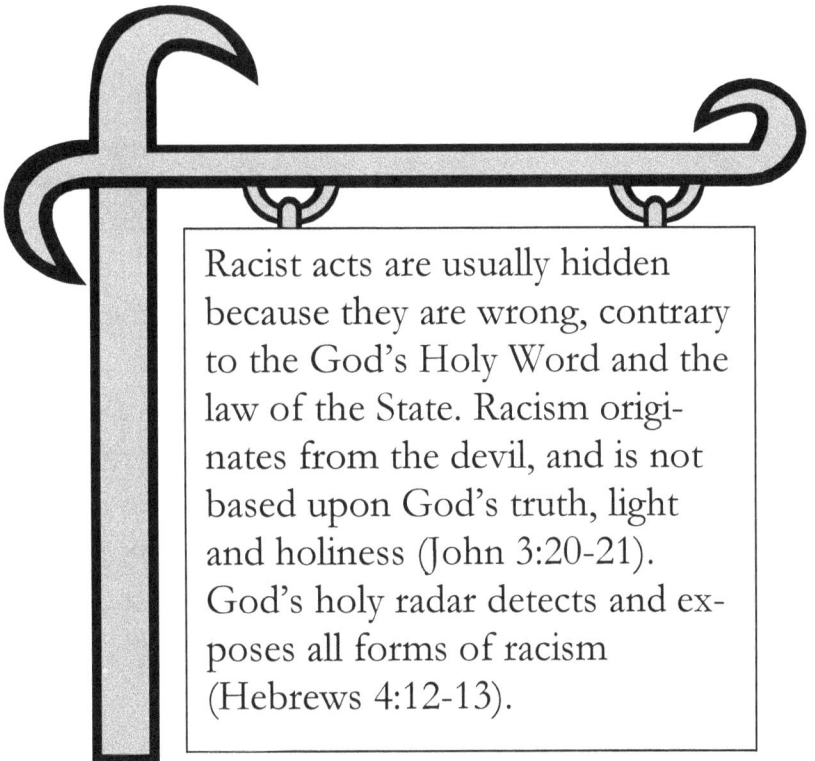

Racist acts are usually hidden because they are wrong, contrary to the God's Holy Word and the law of the State. Racism originates from the devil, and is not based upon God's truth, light and holiness (John 3:20-21). God's holy radar detects and exposes all forms of racism (Hebrews 4:12-13).

62

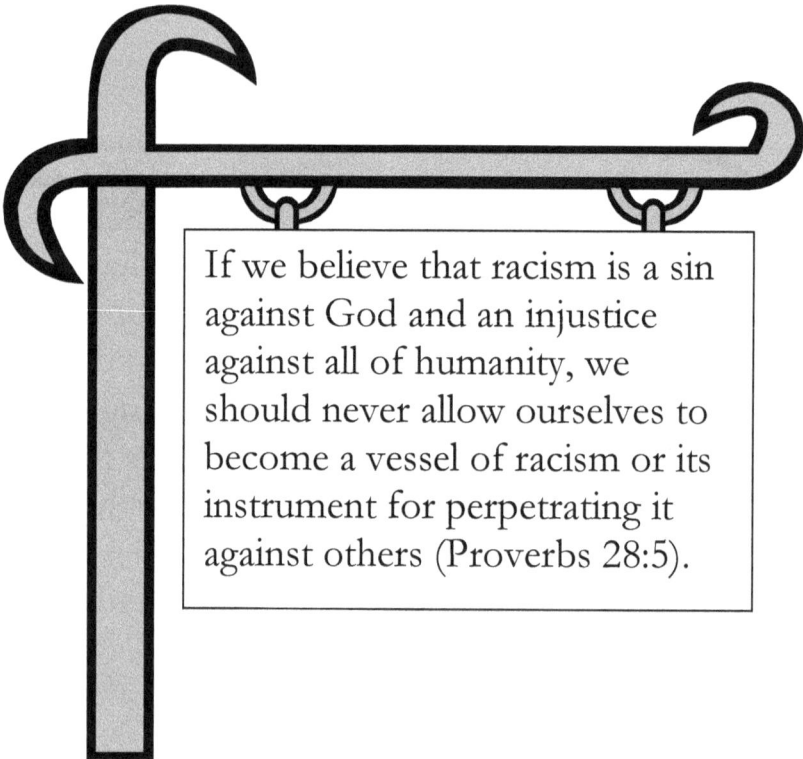

If we believe that racism is a sin against God and an injustice against all of humanity, we should never allow ourselves to become a vessel of racism or its instrument for perpetrating it against others (Proverbs 28:5).

63

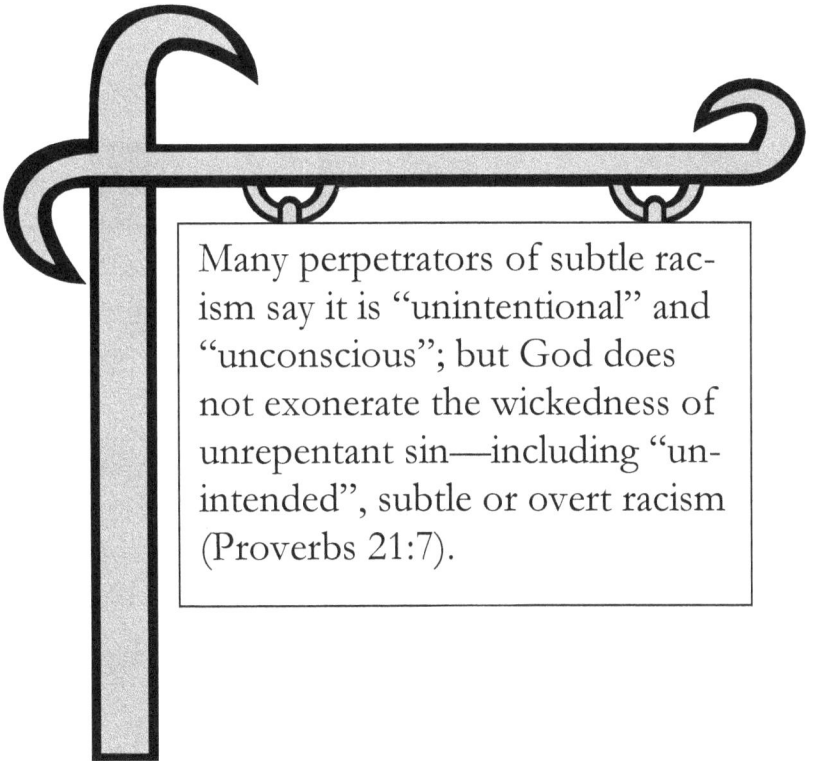

Many perpetrators of subtle racism say it is "unintentional" and "unconscious"; but God does not exonerate the wickedness of unrepentant sin—including "unintended", subtle or overt racism (Proverbs 21:7).

64

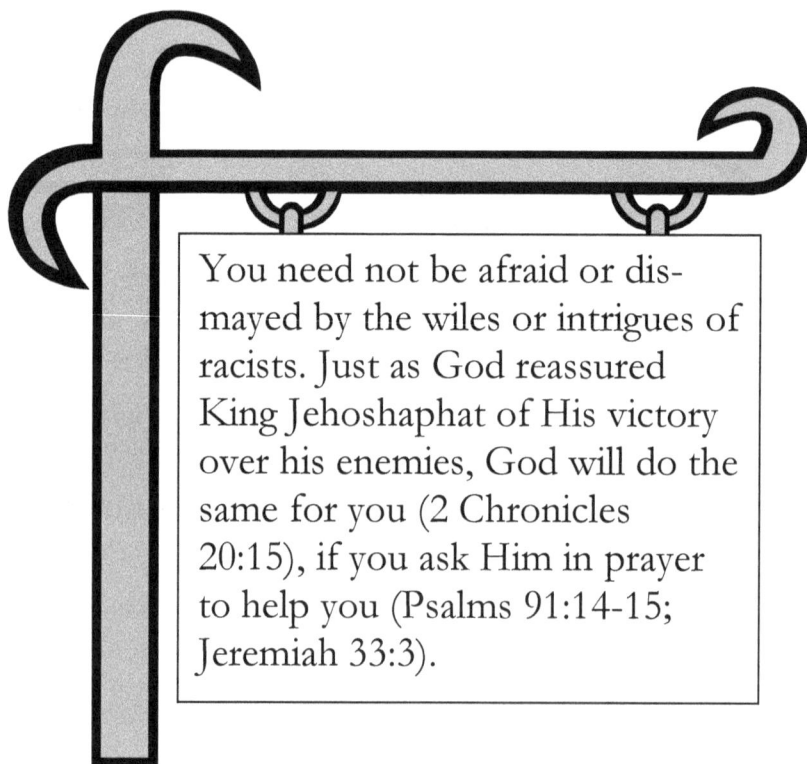

You need not be afraid or dismayed by the wiles or intrigues of racists. Just as God reassured King Jehoshaphat of His victory over his enemies, God will do the same for you (2 Chronicles 20:15), if you ask Him in prayer to help you (Psalms 91:14-15; Jeremiah 33:3).

65

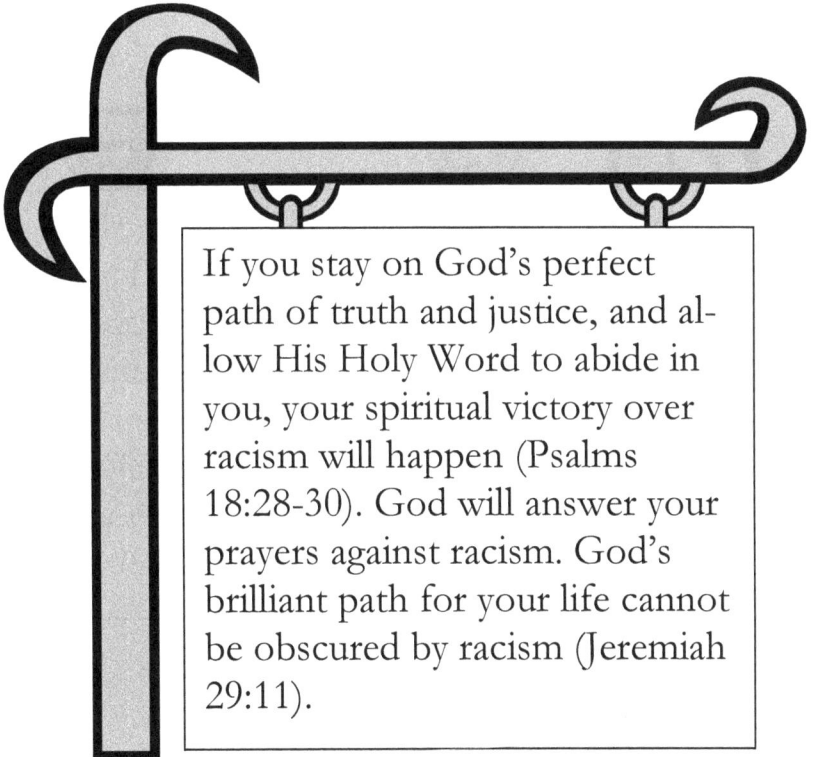

If you stay on God's perfect path of truth and justice, and allow His Holy Word to abide in you, your spiritual victory over racism will happen (Psalms 18:28-30). God will answer your prayers against racism. God's brilliant path for your life cannot be obscured by racism (Jeremiah 29:11).

66

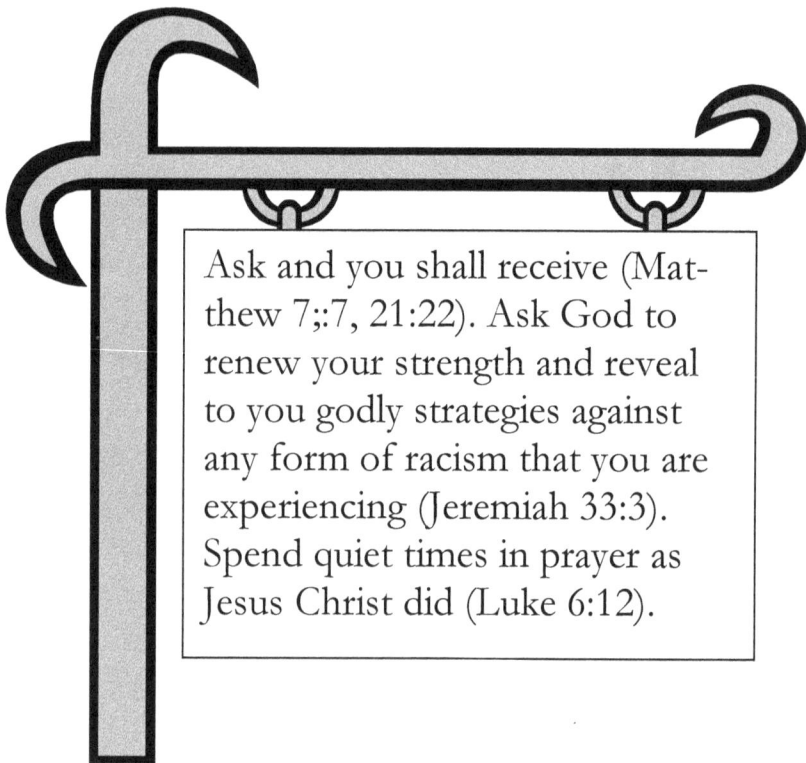

Ask and you shall receive (Matthew 7;:7, 21:22). Ask God to renew your strength and reveal to you godly strategies against any form of racism that you are experiencing (Jeremiah 33:3). Spend quiet times in prayer as Jesus Christ did (Luke 6:12).

67

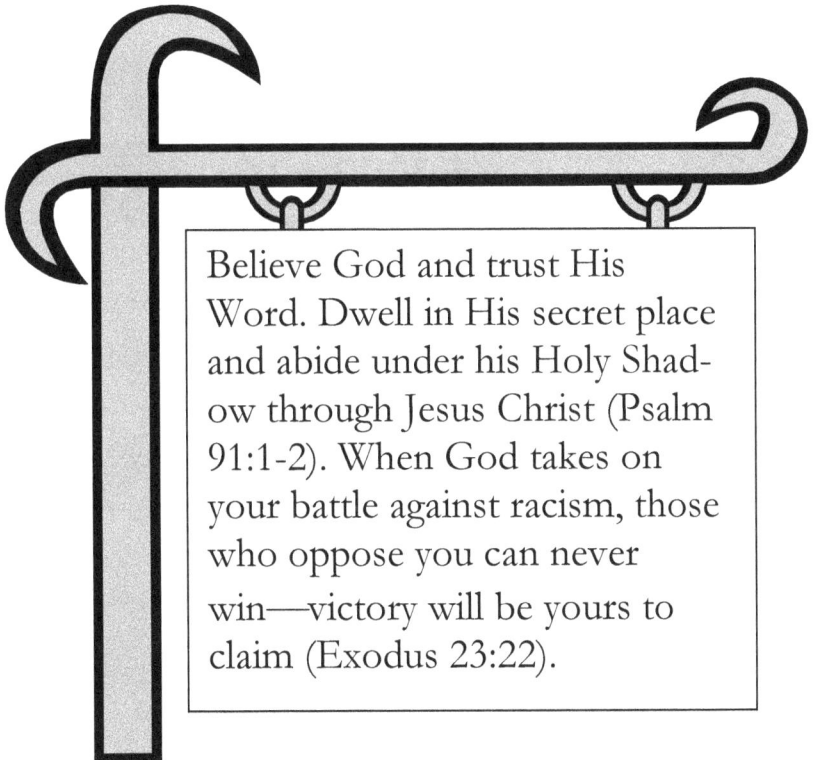

Believe God and trust His Word. Dwell in His secret place and abide under his Holy Shadow through Jesus Christ (Psalm 91:1-2). When God takes on your battle against racism, those who oppose you can never win—victory will be yours to claim (Exodus 23:22).

68

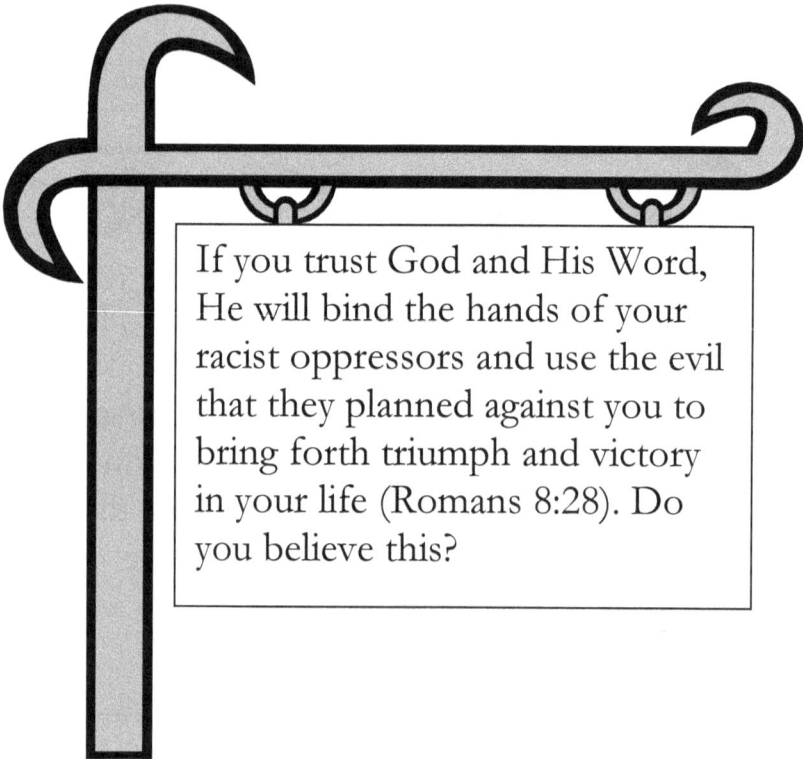

If you trust God and His Word, He will bind the hands of your racist oppressors and use the evil that they planned against you to bring forth triumph and victory in your life (Romans 8:28). Do you believe this?

69

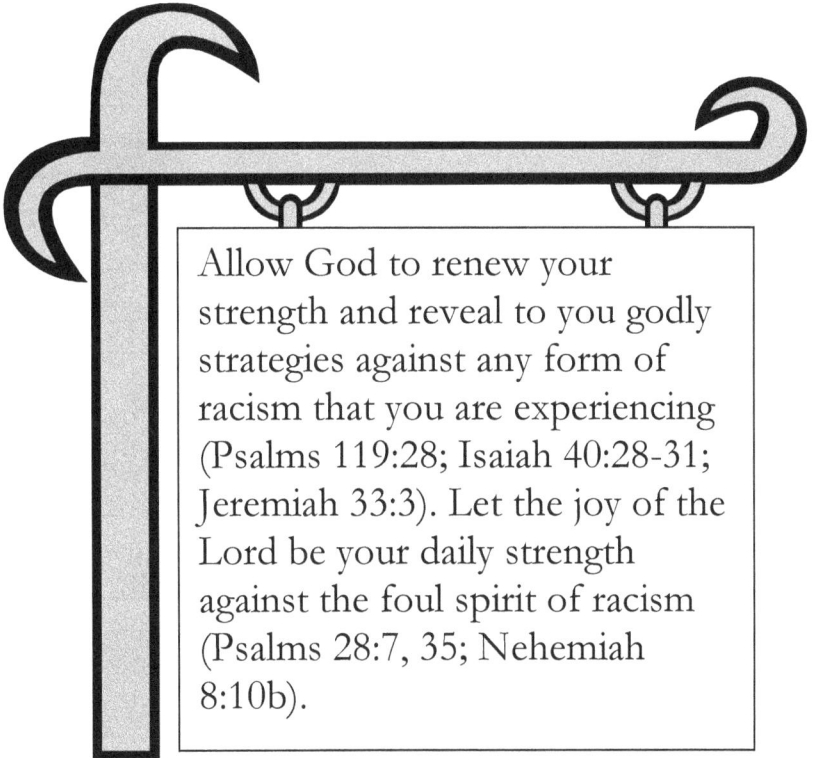

Allow God to renew your strength and reveal to you godly strategies against any form of racism that you are experiencing (Psalms 119:28; Isaiah 40:28-31; Jeremiah 33:3). Let the joy of the Lord be your daily strength against the foul spirit of racism (Psalms 28:7, 35; Nehemiah 8:10b).

70

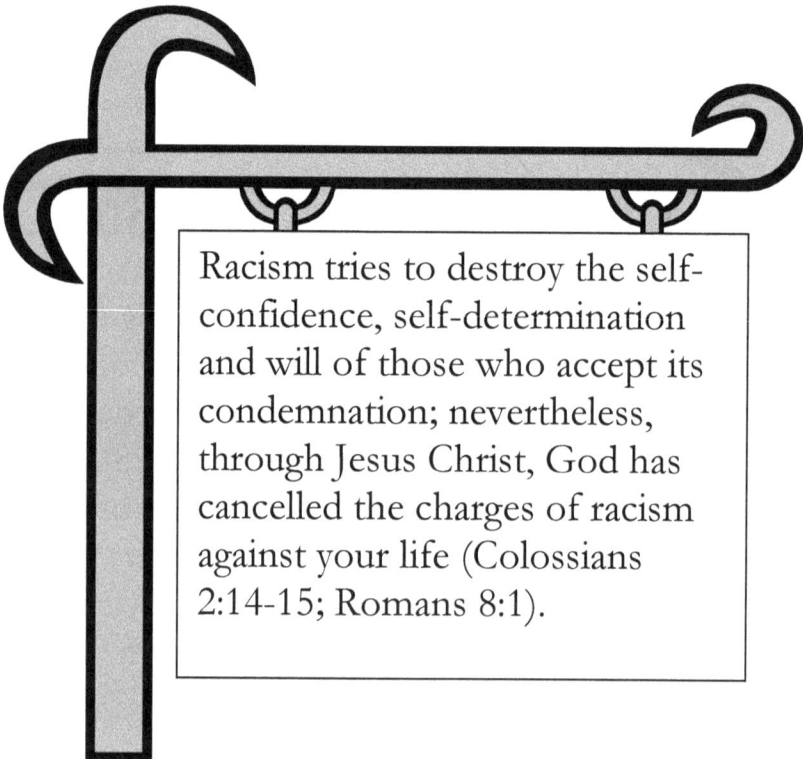

Racism tries to destroy the self-confidence, self-determination and will of those who accept its condemnation; nevertheless, through Jesus Christ, God has cancelled the charges of racism against your life (Colossians 2:14-15; Romans 8:1).

71

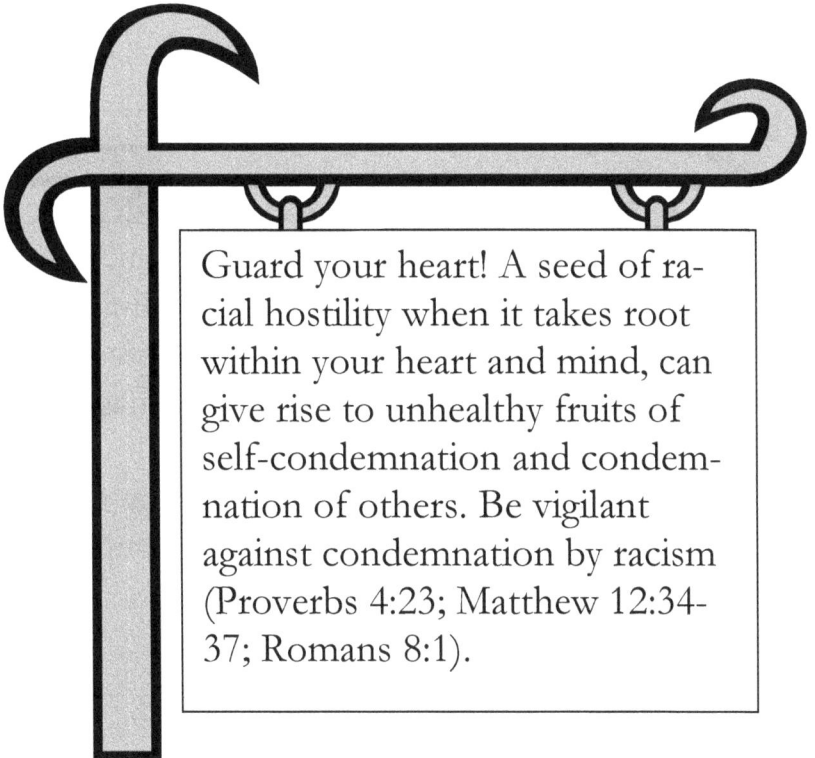

Guard your heart! A seed of racial hostility when it takes root within your heart and mind, can give rise to unhealthy fruits of self-condemnation and condemnation of others. Be vigilant against condemnation by racism (Proverbs 4:23; Matthew 12:34-37; Romans 8:1).

72

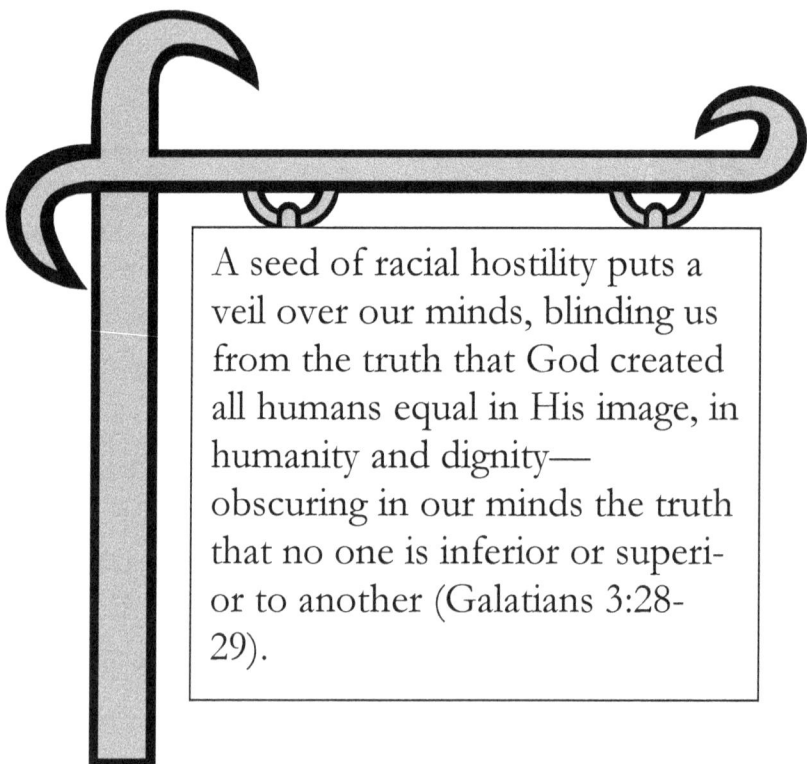

A seed of racial hostility puts a veil over our minds, blinding us from the truth that God created all humans equal in His image, in humanity and dignity—obscuring in our minds the truth that no one is inferior or superior to another (Galatians 3:28-29).

73

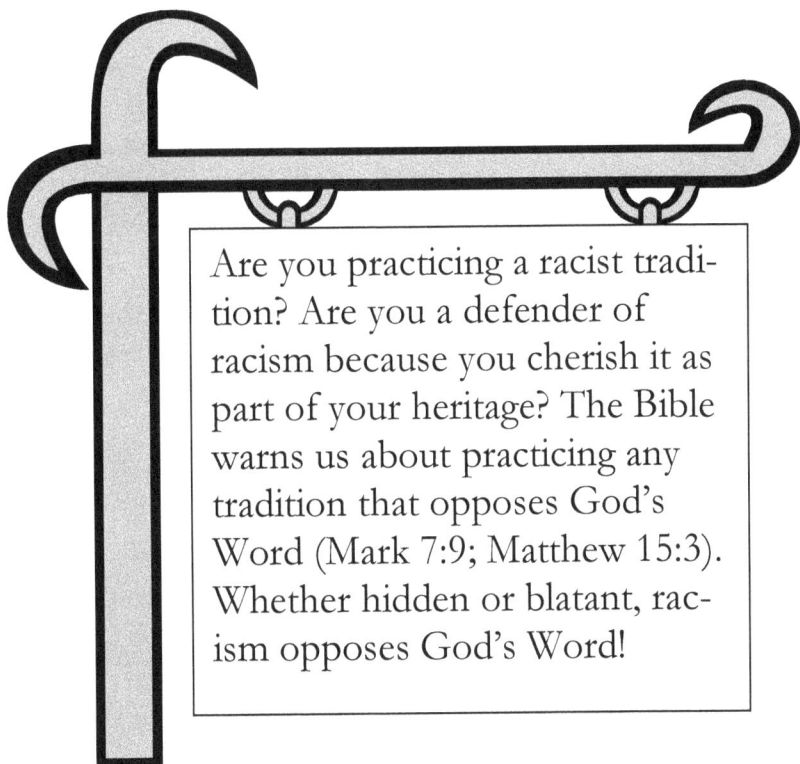

Are you practicing a racist tradition? Are you a defender of racism because you cherish it as part of your heritage? The Bible warns us about practicing any tradition that opposes God's Word (Mark 7:9; Matthew 15:3). Whether hidden or blatant, racism opposes God's Word!

74

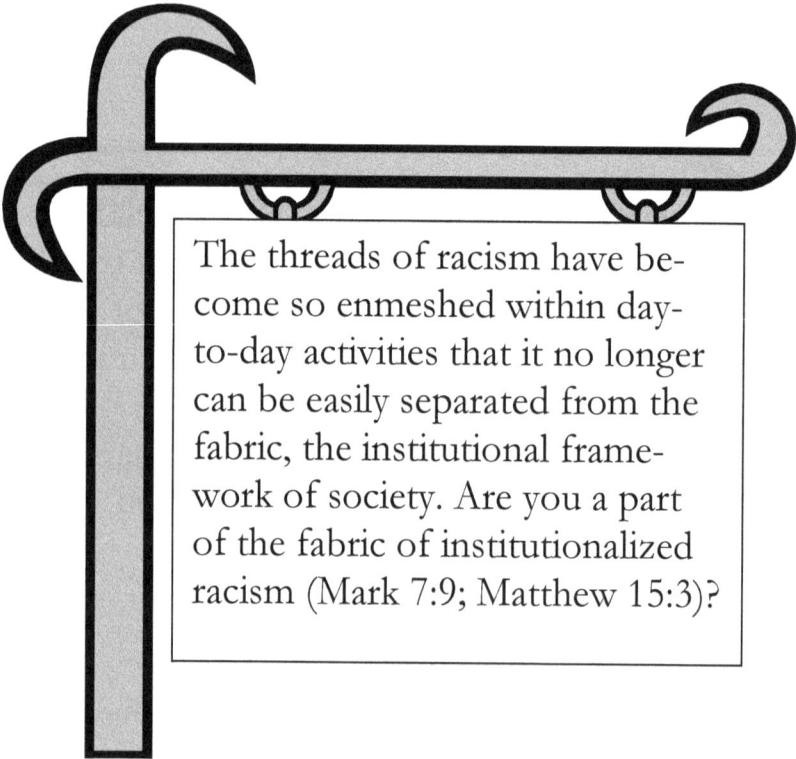

The threads of racism have become so enmeshed within day-to-day activities that it no longer can be easily separated from the fabric, the institutional framework of society. Are you a part of the fabric of institutionalized racism (Mark 7:9; Matthew 15:3)?

75

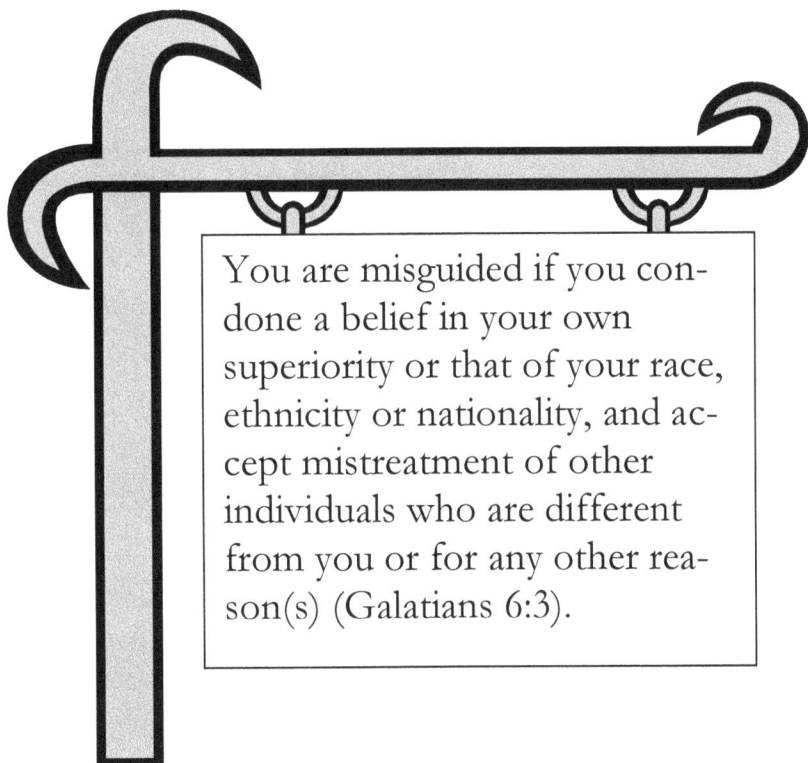

You are misguided if you condone a belief in your own superiority or that of your race, ethnicity or nationality, and accept mistreatment of other individuals who are different from you or for any other reason(s) (Galatians 6:3).

76

God corrected Apostle Peter's racial bias so that the foul spirit of racism would not taint his heart (Acts 10:27-29). What about you? Do you condone subtle or overt racism? God's Word has specifically instructed us not to conform to ungodly traditions of the world (Romans 12:2).

77

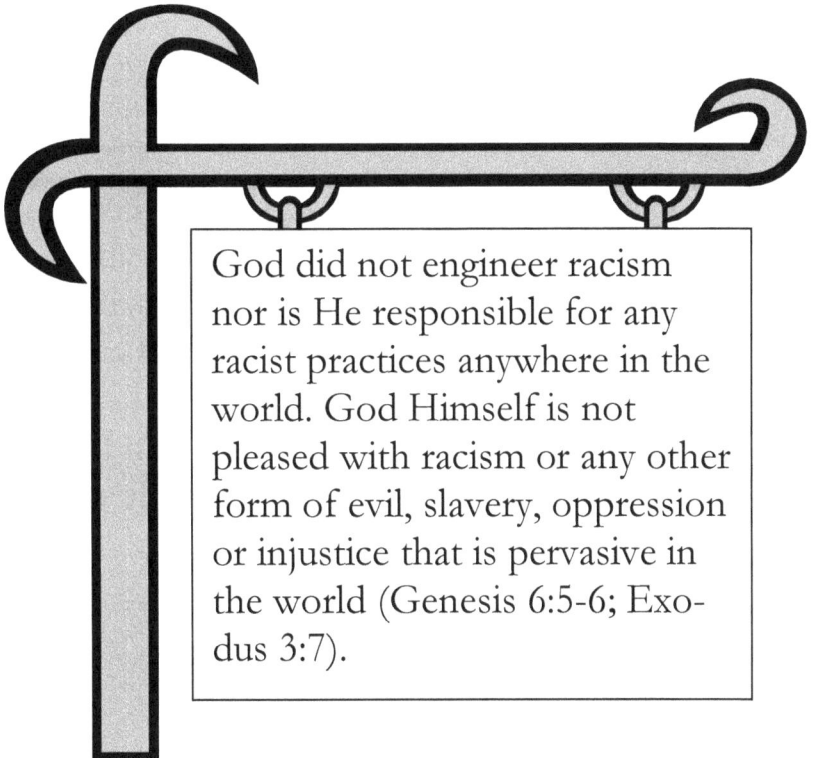

God did not engineer racism nor is He responsible for any racist practices anywhere in the world. God Himself is not pleased with racism or any other form of evil, slavery, oppression or injustice that is pervasive in the world (Genesis 6:5-6; Exodus 3:7).

78

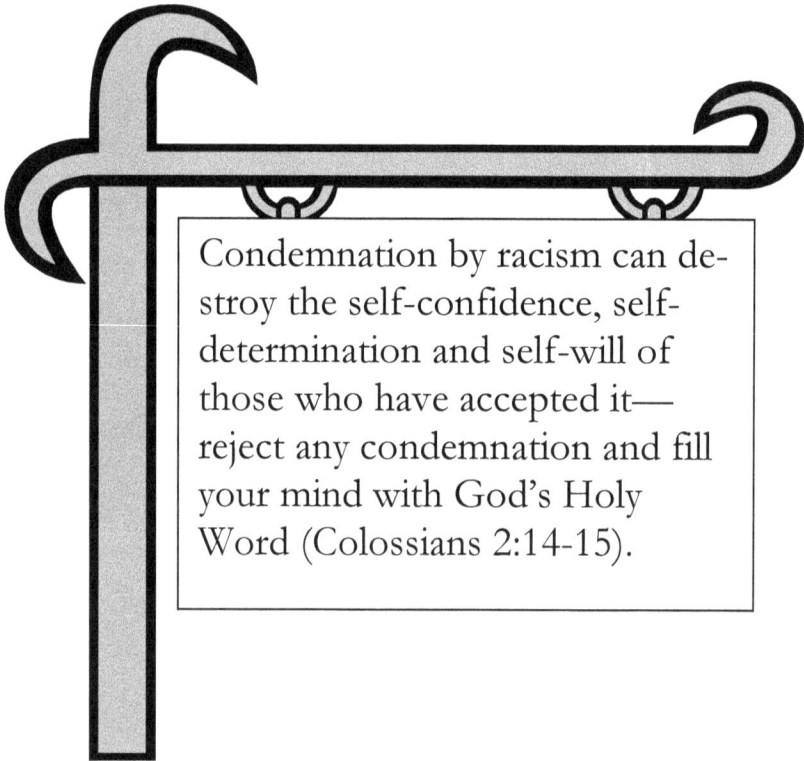

Condemnation by racism can destroy the self-confidence, self-determination and self-will of those who have accepted it—reject any condemnation and fill your mind with God's Holy Word (Colossians 2:14-15).

79

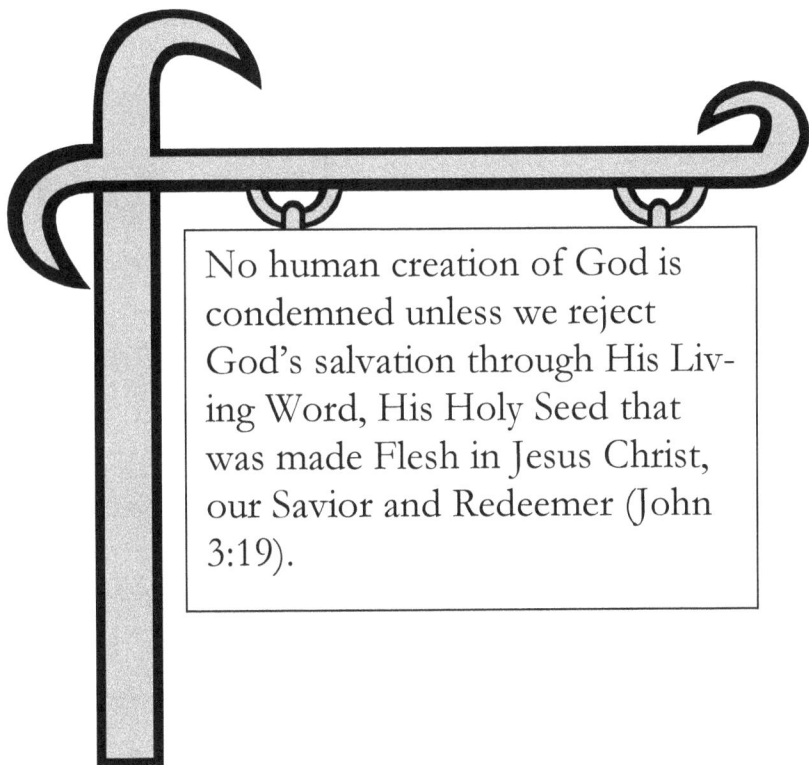

No human creation of God is condemned unless we reject God's salvation through His Living Word, His Holy Seed that was made Flesh in Jesus Christ, our Savior and Redeemer (John 3:19).

80

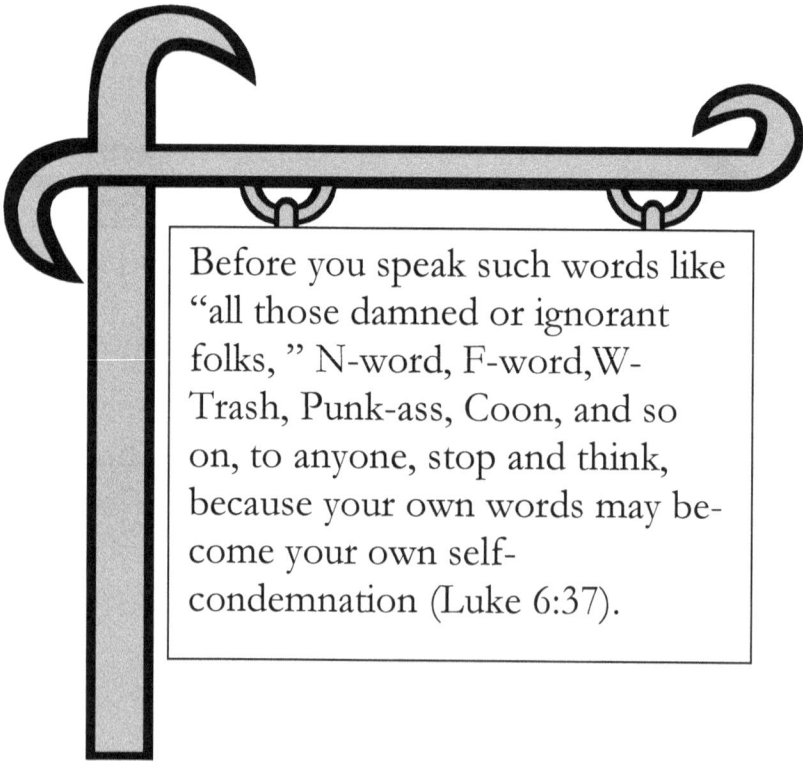

Before you speak such words like "all those damned or ignorant folks, " N-word, F-word, W-Trash, Punk-ass, Coon, and so on, to anyone, stop and think, because your own words may become your own self-condemnation (Luke 6:37).

81

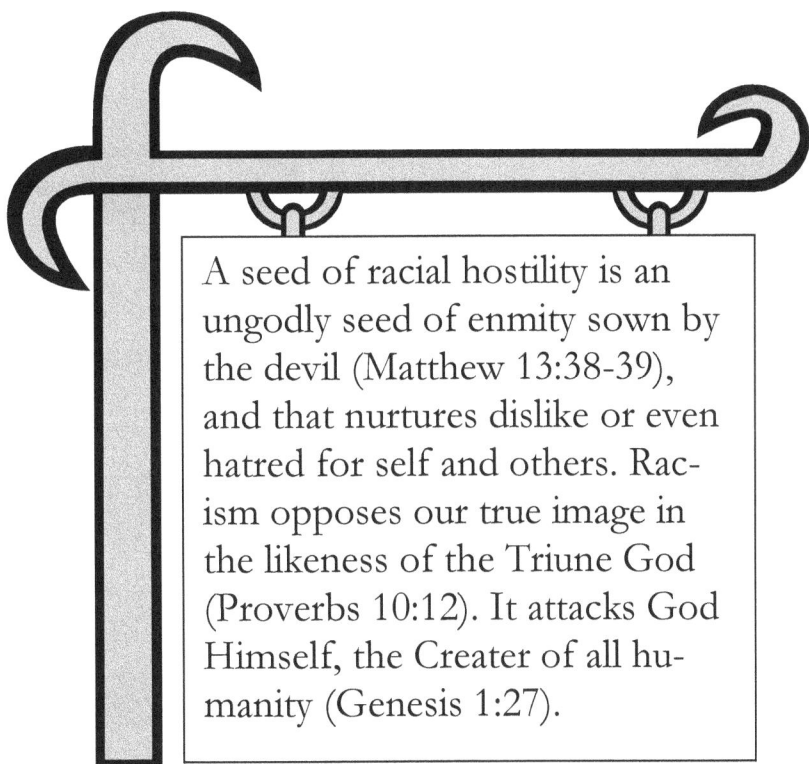

A seed of racial hostility is an ungodly seed of enmity sown by the devil (Matthew 13:38-39), and that nurtures dislike or even hatred for self and others. Racism opposes our true image in the likeness of the Triune God (Proverbs 10:12). It attacks God Himself, the Creater of all humanity (Genesis 1:27).

82

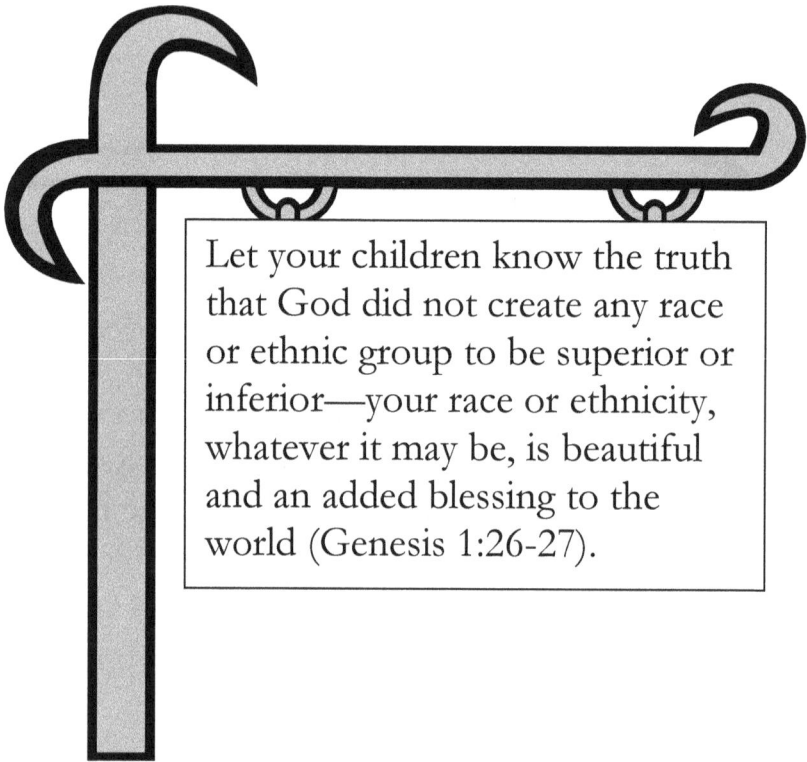

Let your children know the truth that God did not create any race or ethnic group to be superior or inferior—your race or ethnicity, whatever it may be, is beautiful and an added blessing to the world (Genesis 1:26-27).

83

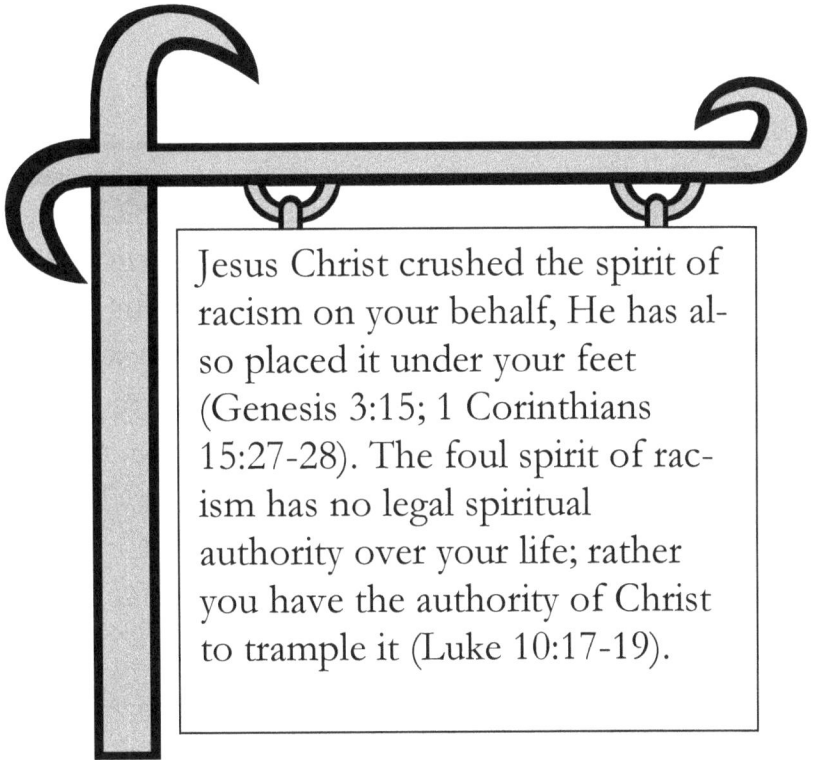

Jesus Christ crushed the spirit of racism on your behalf, He has also placed it under your feet (Genesis 3:15; 1 Corinthians 15:27-28). The foul spirit of racism has no legal spiritual authority over your life; rather you have the authority of Christ to trample it (Luke 10:17-19).

84

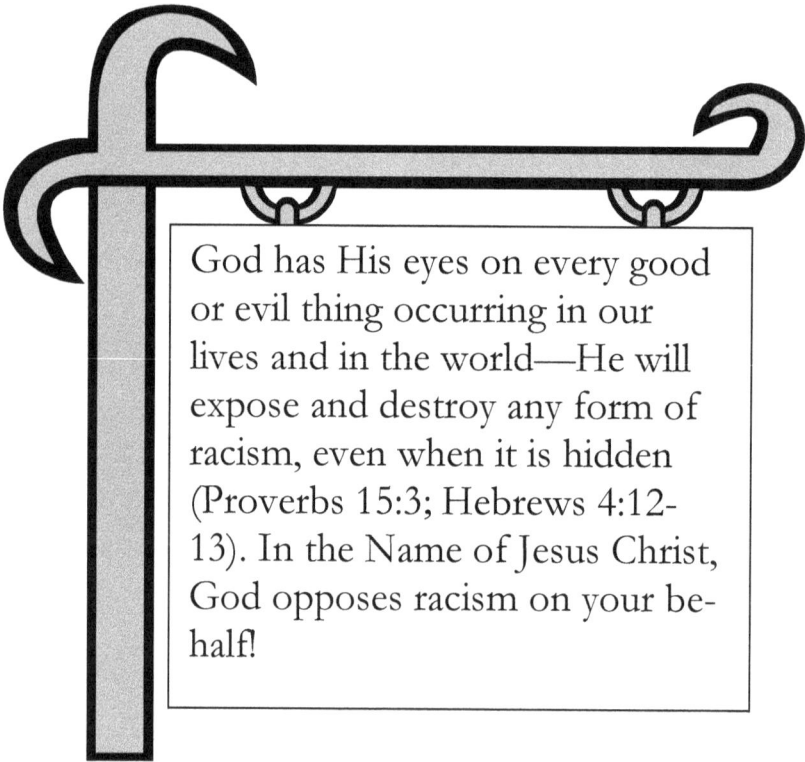

God has His eyes on every good or evil thing occurring in our lives and in the world—He will expose and destroy any form of racism, even when it is hidden (Proverbs 15:3; Hebrews 4:12-13). In the Name of Jesus Christ, God opposes racism on your behalf!

85

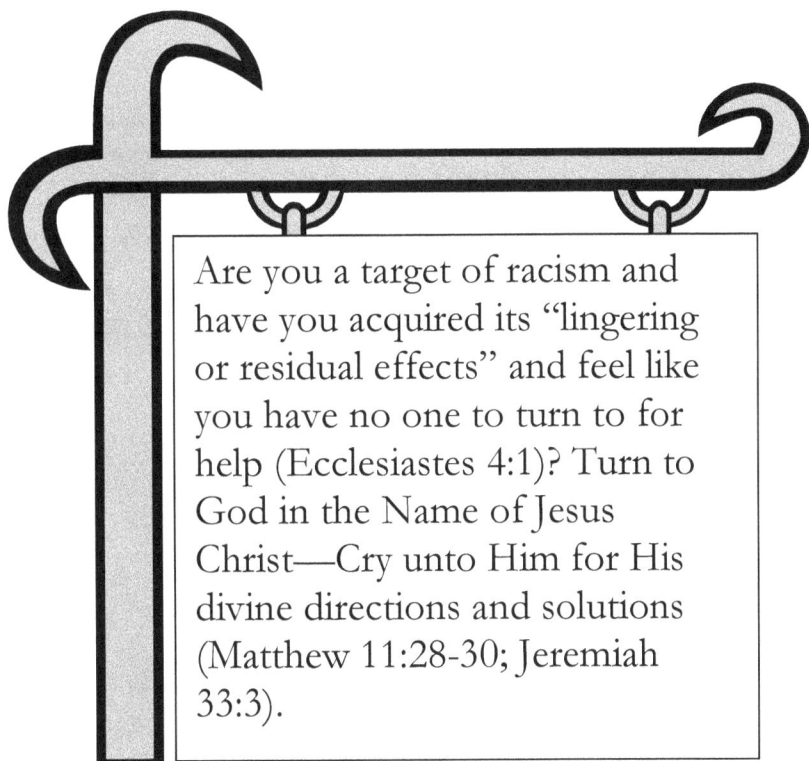

Are you a target of racism and have you acquired its "lingering or residual effects" and feel like you have no one to turn to for help (Ecclesiastes 4:1)? Turn to God in the Name of Jesus Christ—Cry unto Him for His divine directions and solutions (Matthew 11:28-30; Jeremiah 33:3).

86

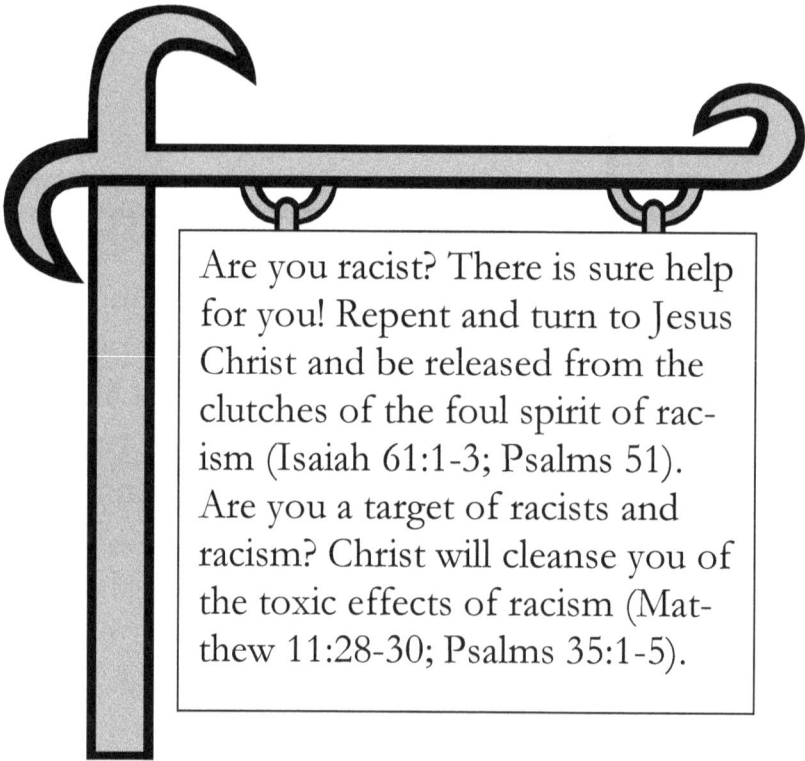

Are you racist? There is sure help for you! Repent and turn to Jesus Christ and be released from the clutches of the foul spirit of racism (Isaiah 61:1-3; Psalms 51). Are you a target of racists and racism? Christ will cleanse you of the toxic effects of racism (Matthew 11:28-30; Psalms 35:1-5).

87

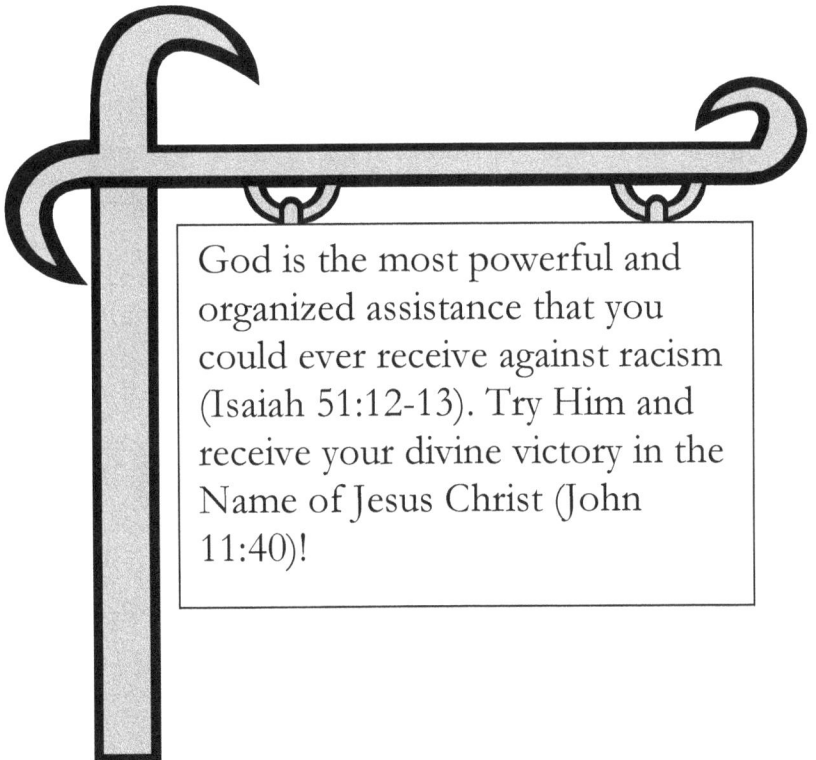

God is the most powerful and organized assistance that you could ever receive against racism (Isaiah 51:12-13). Try Him and receive your divine victory in the Name of Jesus Christ (John 11:40)!

88

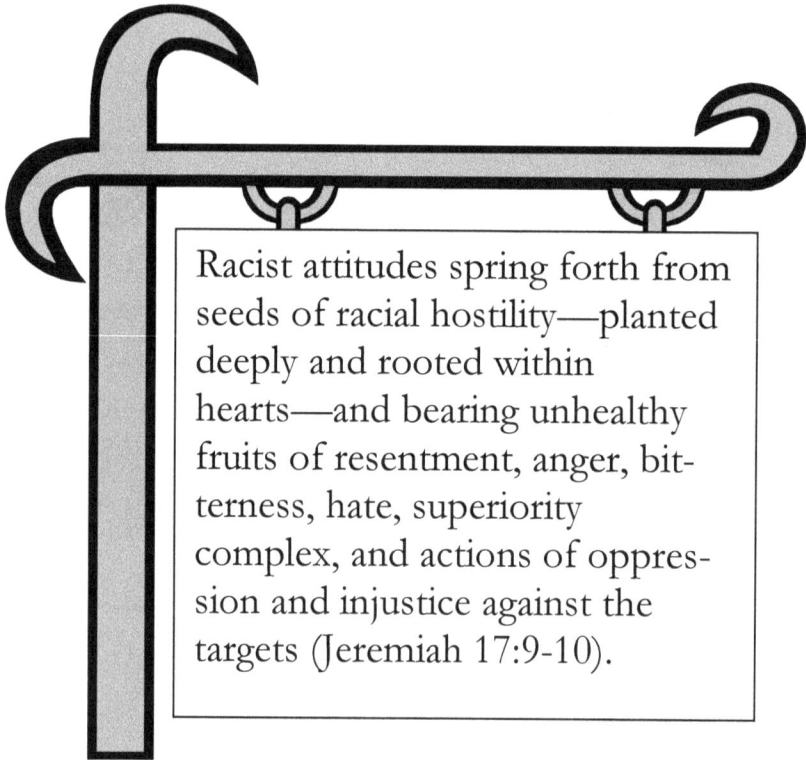

Racist attitudes spring forth from seeds of racial hostility—planted deeply and rooted within hearts—and bearing unhealthy fruits of resentment, anger, bitterness, hate, superiority complex, and actions of oppression and injustice against the targets (Jeremiah 17:9-10).

89

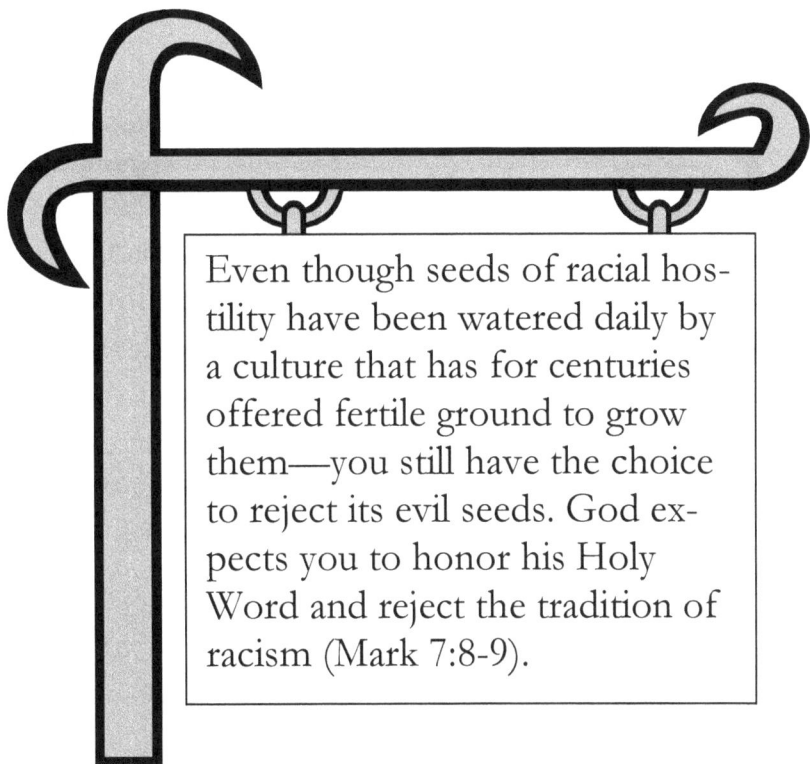

Even though seeds of racial hostility have been watered daily by a culture that has for centuries offered fertile ground to grow them—you still have the choice to reject its evil seeds. God expects you to honor his Holy Word and reject the tradition of racism (Mark 7:8-9).

90

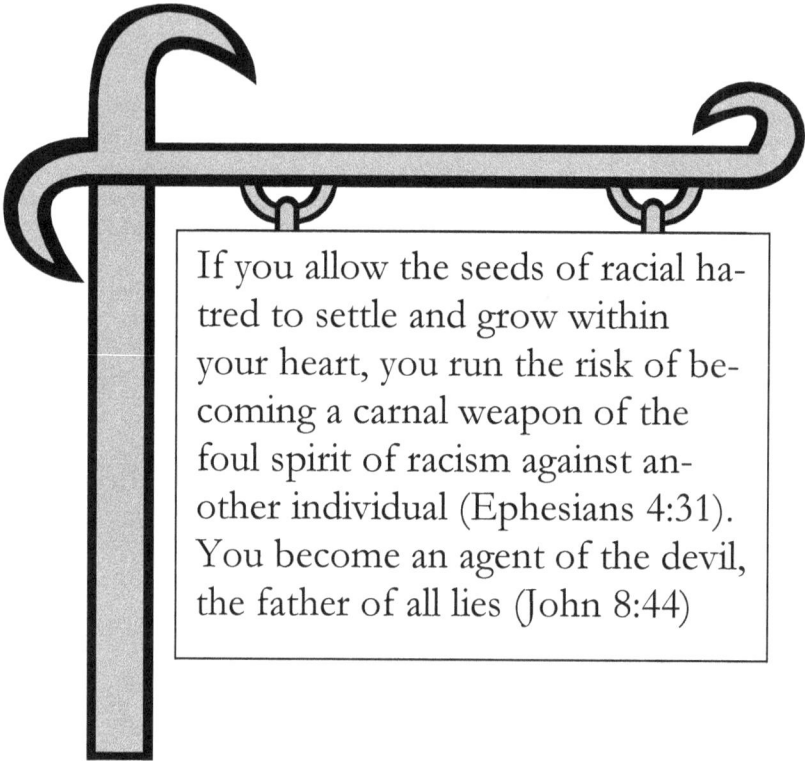

If you allow the seeds of racial hatred to settle and grow within your heart, you run the risk of becoming a carnal weapon of the foul spirit of racism against another individual (Ephesians 4:31). You become an agent of the devil, the father of all lies (John 8:44)

91

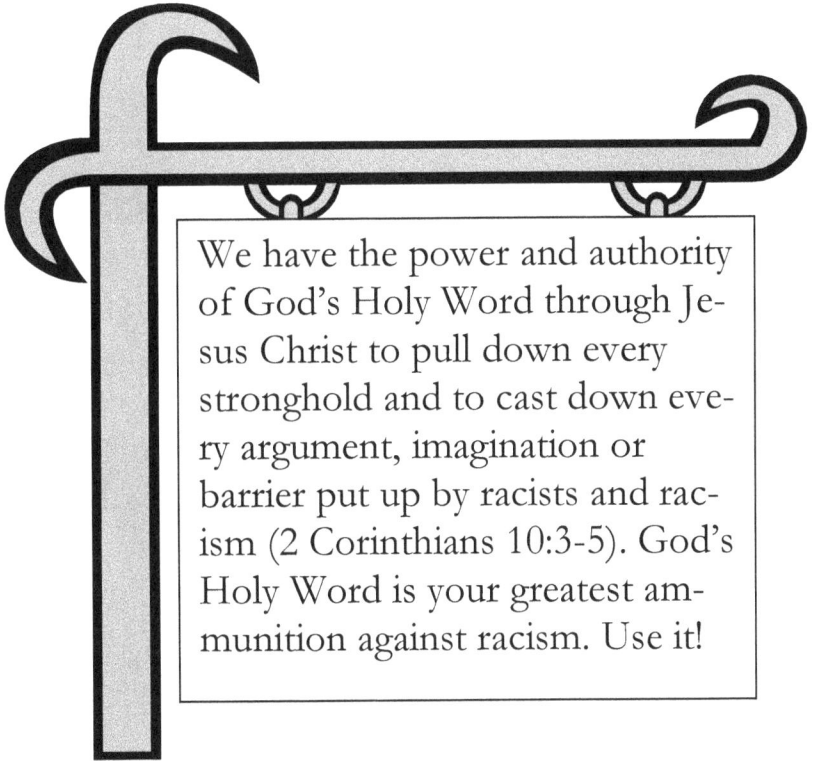

We have the power and authority of God's Holy Word through Jesus Christ to pull down every stronghold and to cast down every argument, imagination or barrier put up by racists and racism (2 Corinthians 10:3-5). God's Holy Word is your greatest ammunition against racism. Use it!

92

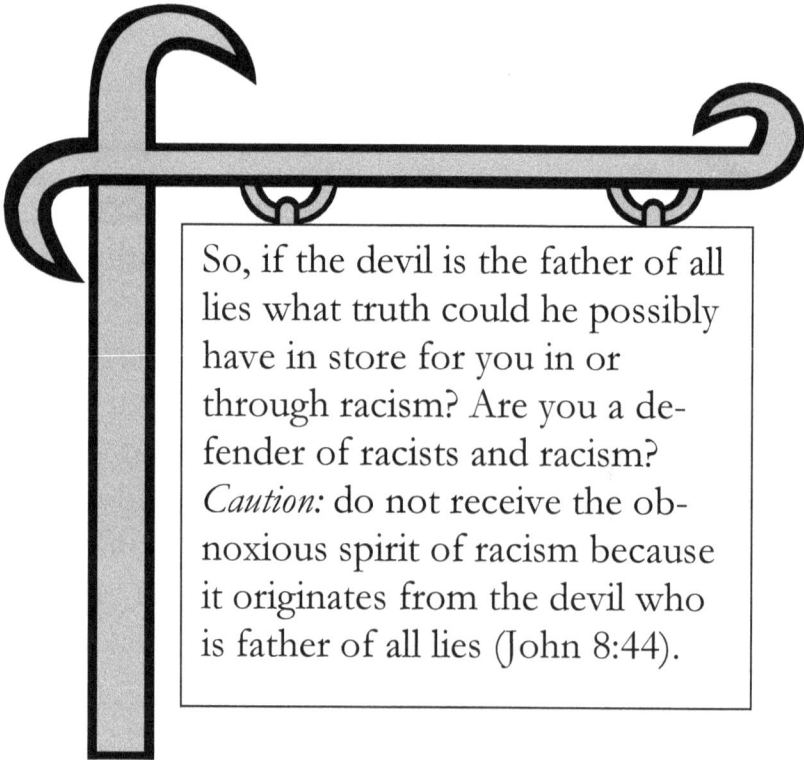

So, if the devil is the father of all lies what truth could he possibly have in store for you in or through racism? Are you a defender of racists and racism? *Caution:* do not receive the obnoxious spirit of racism because it originates from the devil who is father of all lies (John 8:44).

93

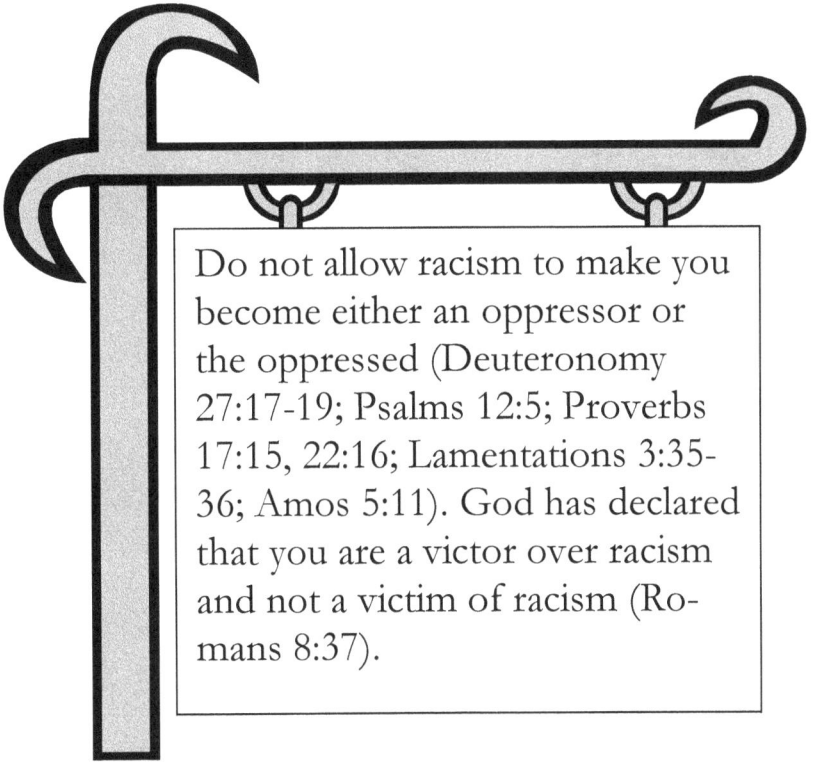

Do not allow racism to make you become either an oppressor or the oppressed (Deuteronomy 27:17-19; Psalms 12:5; Proverbs 17:15, 22:16; Lamentations 3:35-36; Amos 5:11). God has declared that you are a victor over racism and not a victim of racism (Romans 8:37).

94

If you allow your soul to be oppressed by racism, you will become a "toy" for the devil to misuse (1 Peter 5:8). Reject racism! Racism is a demonic spirit of oppression which comes from the devil, the father of all lies (John 8:44).

95

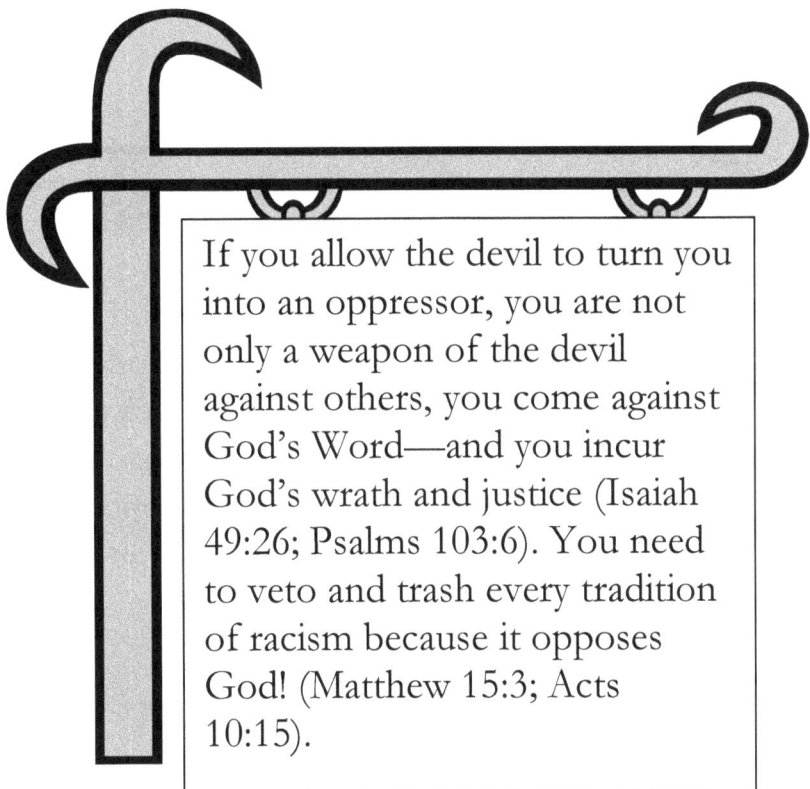

If you allow the devil to turn you into an oppressor, you are not only a weapon of the devil against others, you come against God's Word—and you incur God's wrath and justice (Isaiah 49:26; Psalms 103:6). You need to veto and trash every tradition of racism because it opposes God! (Matthew 15:3; Acts 10:15).

96

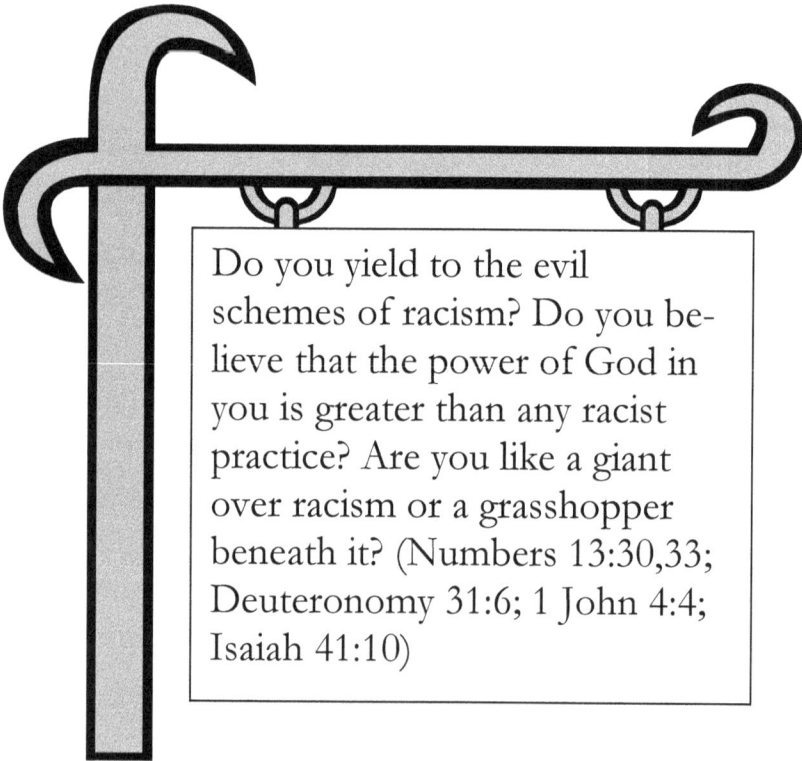

Do you yield to the evil schemes of racism? Do you believe that the power of God in you is greater than any racist practice? Are you like a giant over racism or a grasshopper beneath it? (Numbers 13:30,33; Deuteronomy 31:6; 1 John 4:4; Isaiah 41:10)

97

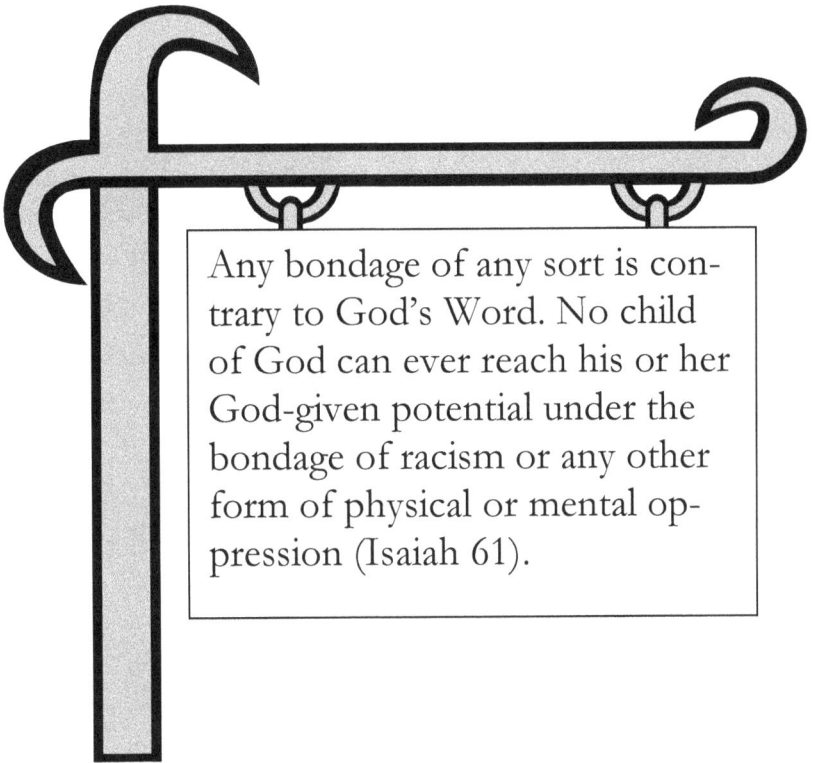

Any bondage of any sort is contrary to God's Word. No child of God can ever reach his or her God-given potential under the bondage of racism or any other form of physical or mental oppression (Isaiah 61).

98

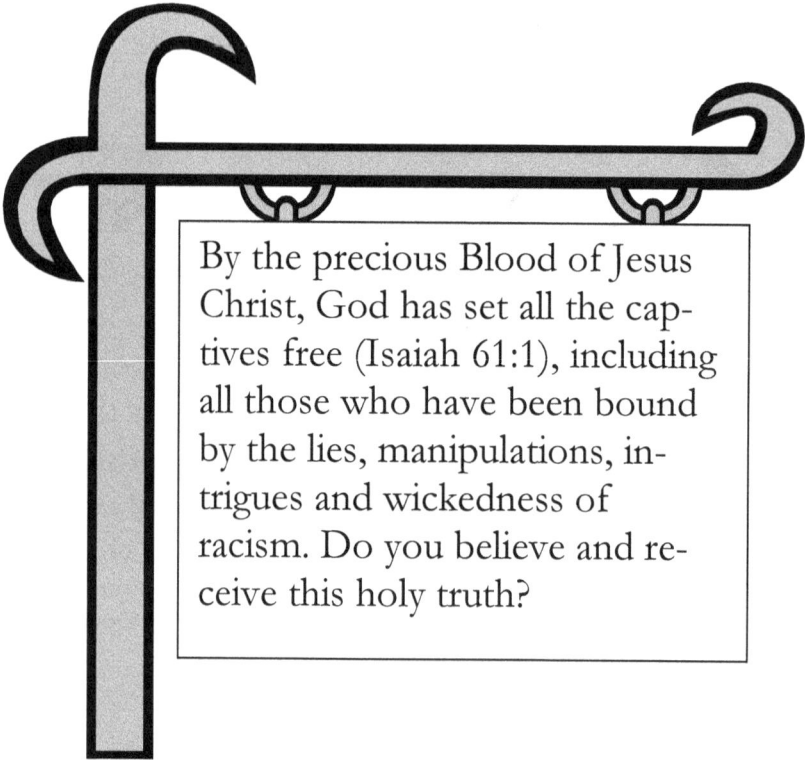

By the precious Blood of Jesus Christ, God has set all the captives free (Isaiah 61:1), including all those who have been bound by the lies, manipulations, intrigues and wickedness of racism. Do you believe and receive this holy truth?

99

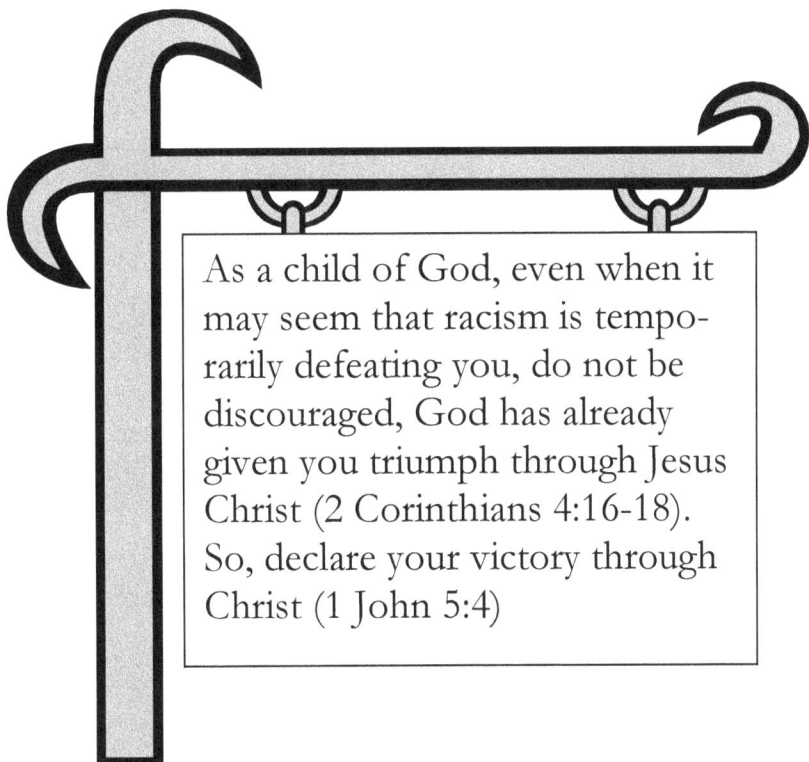

As a child of God, even when it may seem that racism is temporarily defeating you, do not be discouraged, God has already given you triumph through Jesus Christ (2 Corinthians 4:16-18). So, declare your victory through Christ (1 John 5:4)

100

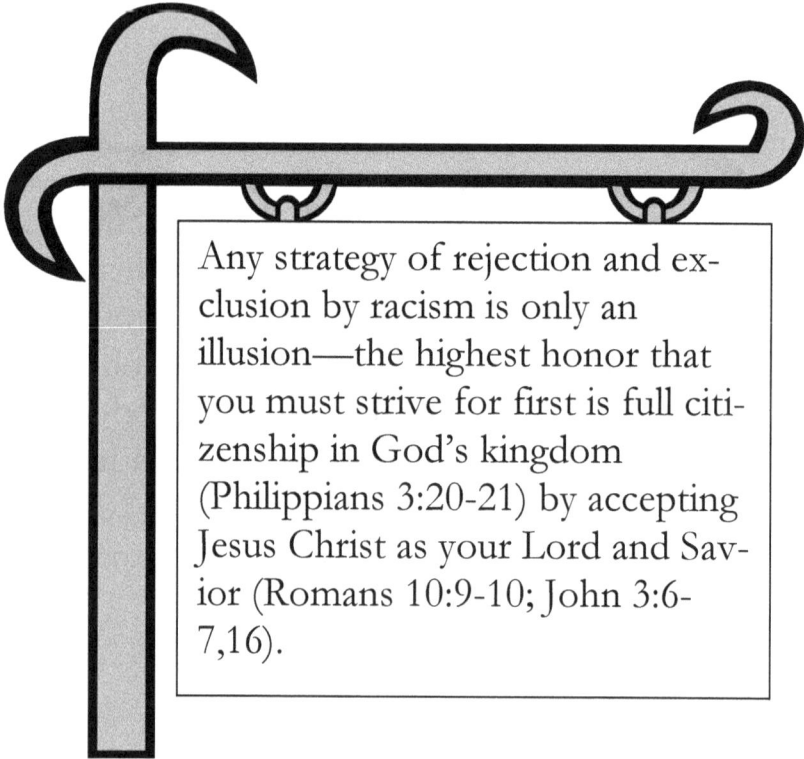

Any strategy of rejection and exclusion by racism is only an illusion—the highest honor that you must strive for first is full citizenship in God's kingdom (Philippians 3:20-21) by accepting Jesus Christ as your Lord and Savior (Romans 10:9-10; John 3:6-7,16).

101

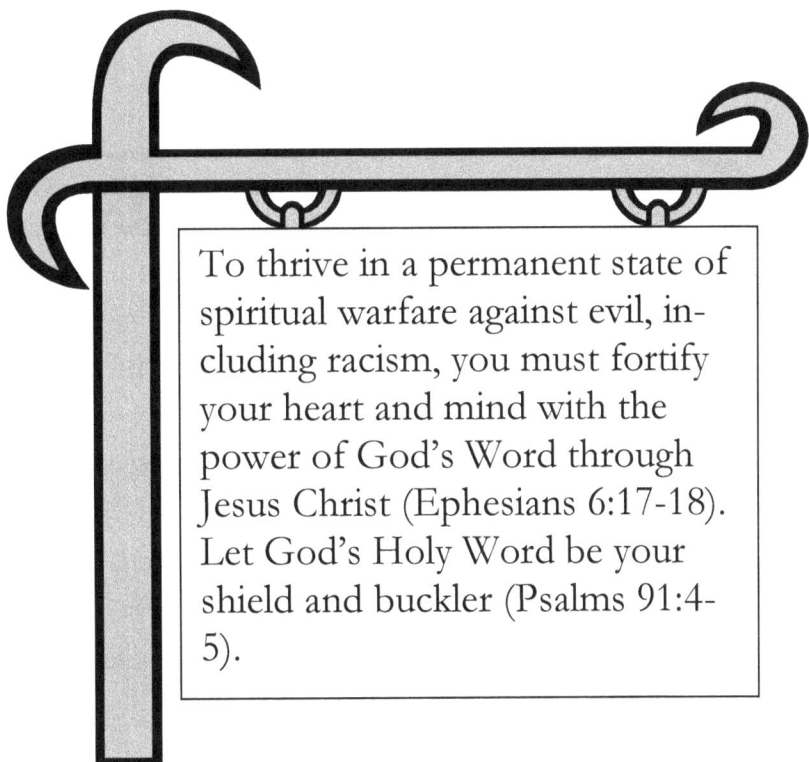

To thrive in a permanent state of spiritual warfare against evil, including racism, you must fortify your heart and mind with the power of God's Word through Jesus Christ (Ephesians 6:17-18). Let God's Holy Word be your shield and buckler (Psalms 91:4-5).

102

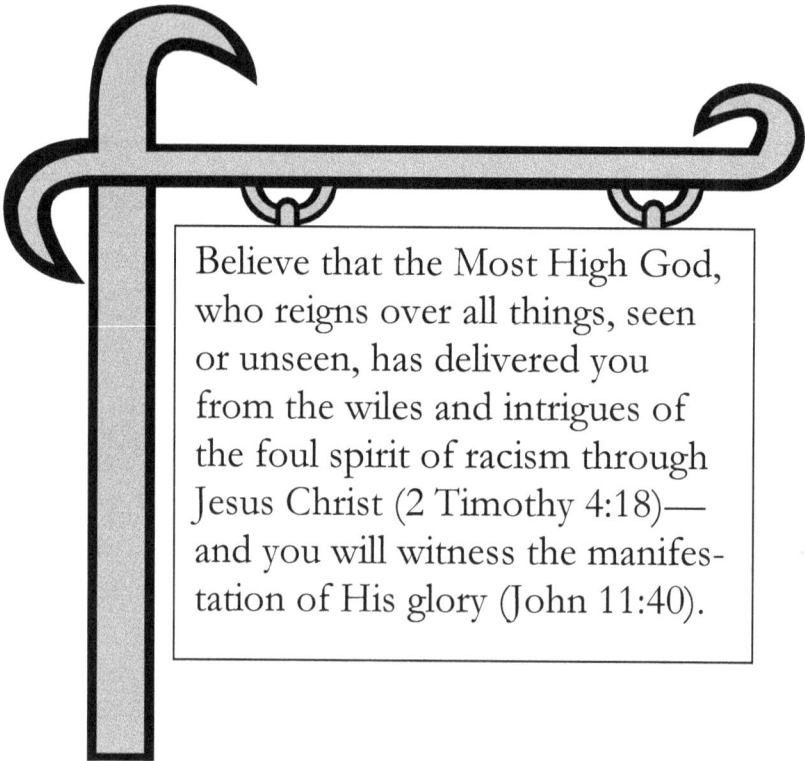

Believe that the Most High God, who reigns over all things, seen or unseen, has delivered you from the wiles and intrigues of the foul spirit of racism through Jesus Christ (2 Timothy 4:18)— and you will witness the manifestation of His glory (John 11:40).

103

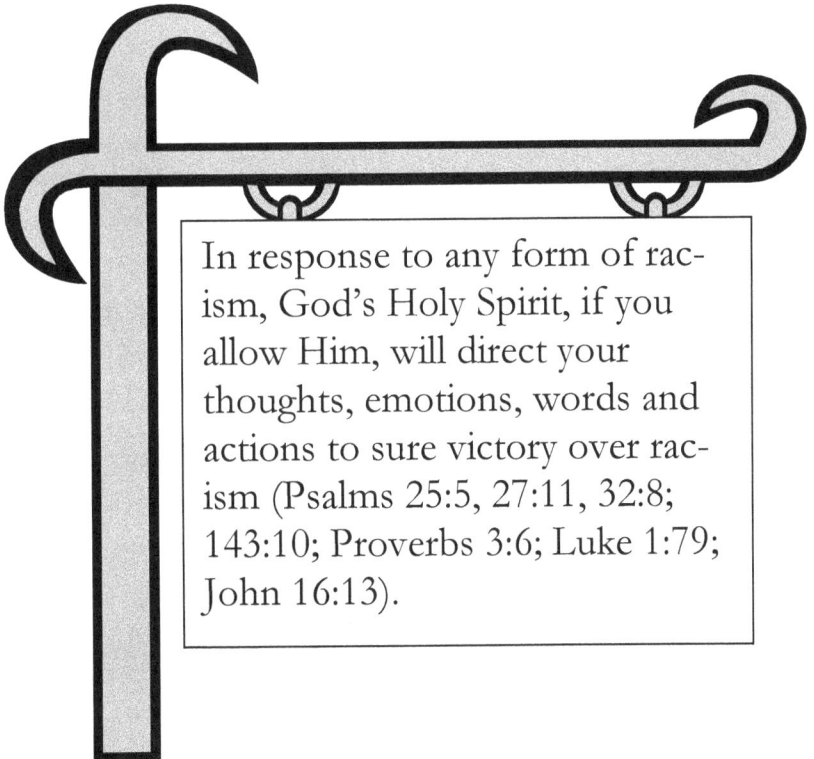

In response to any form of racism, God's Holy Spirit, if you allow Him, will direct your thoughts, emotions, words and actions to sure victory over racism (Psalms 25:5, 27:11, 32:8; 143:10; Proverbs 3:6; Luke 1:79; John 16:13).

104

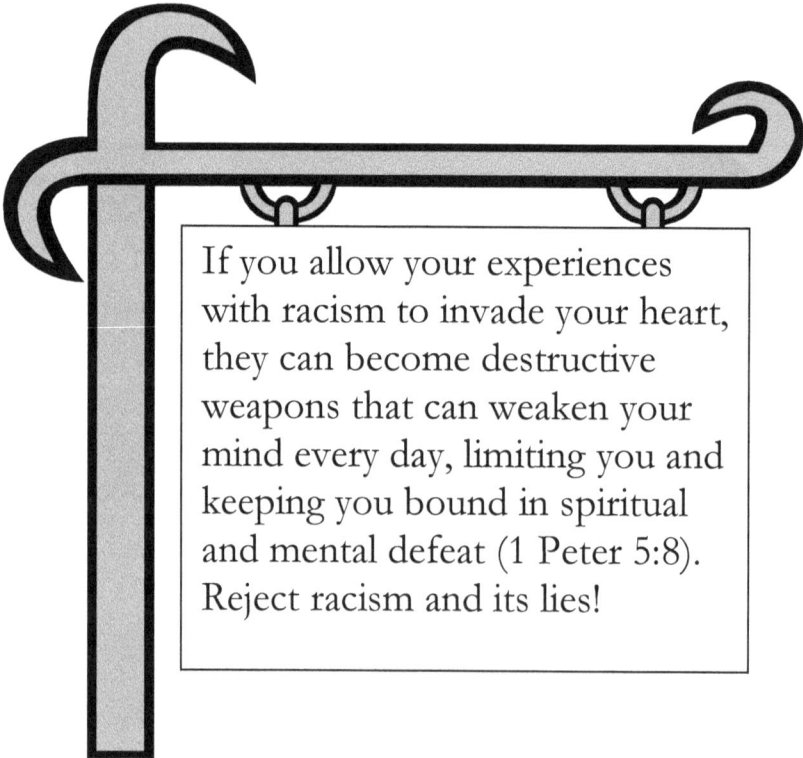

If you allow your experiences with racism to invade your heart, they can become destructive weapons that can weaken your mind every day, limiting you and keeping you bound in spiritual and mental defeat (1 Peter 5:8). Reject racism and its lies!

105

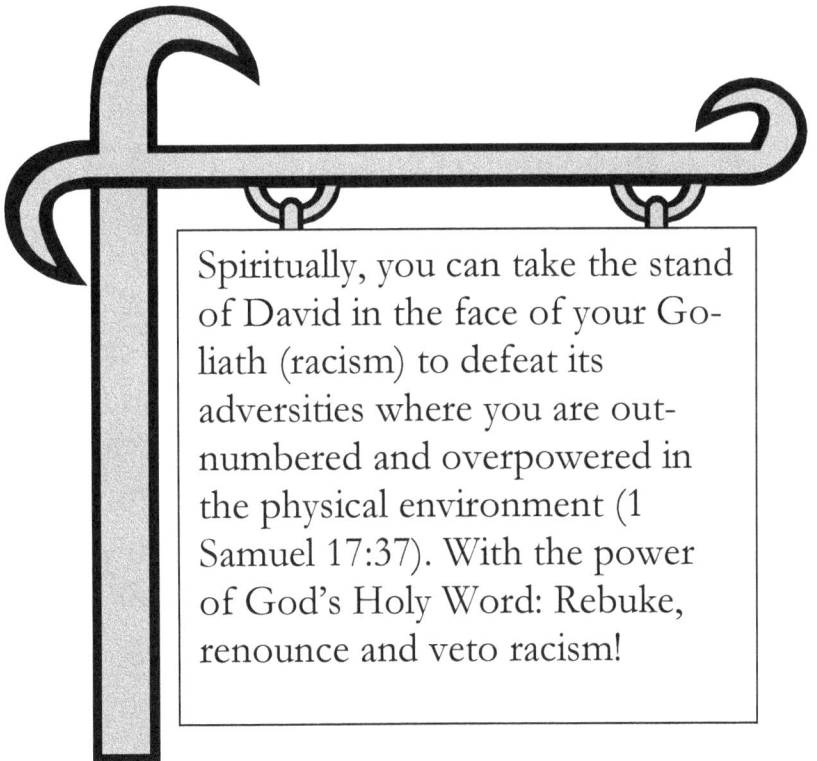

Spiritually, you can take the stand of David in the face of your Goliath (racism) to defeat its adversities where you are outnumbered and overpowered in the physical environment (1 Samuel 17:37). With the power of God's Holy Word: Rebuke, renounce and veto racism!

106

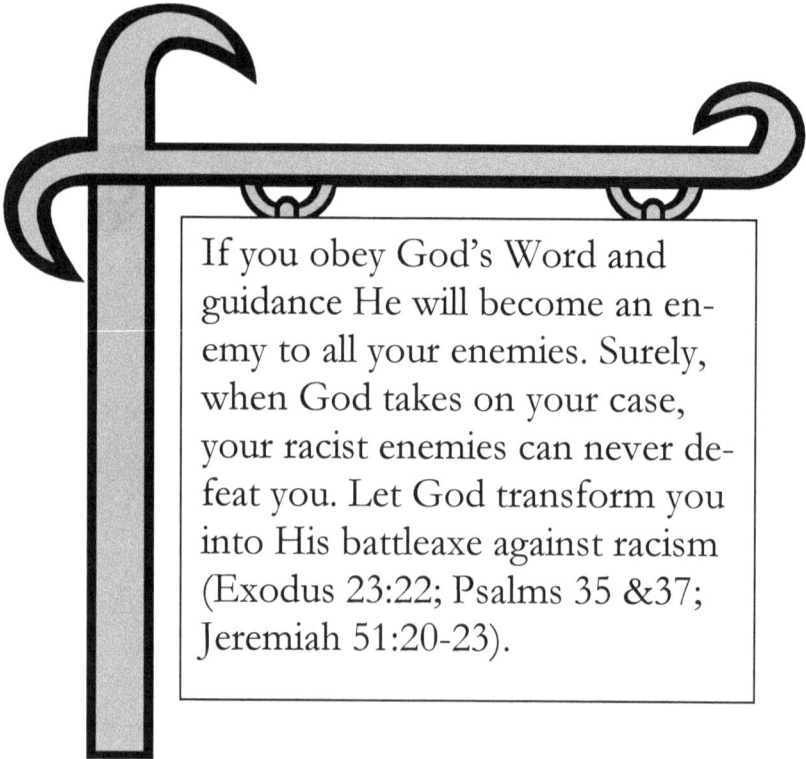

If you obey God's Word and guidance He will become an enemy to all your enemies. Surely, when God takes on your case, your racist enemies can never defeat you. Let God transform you into His battleaxe against racism (Exodus 23:22; Psalms 35 &37; Jeremiah 51:20-23).

107

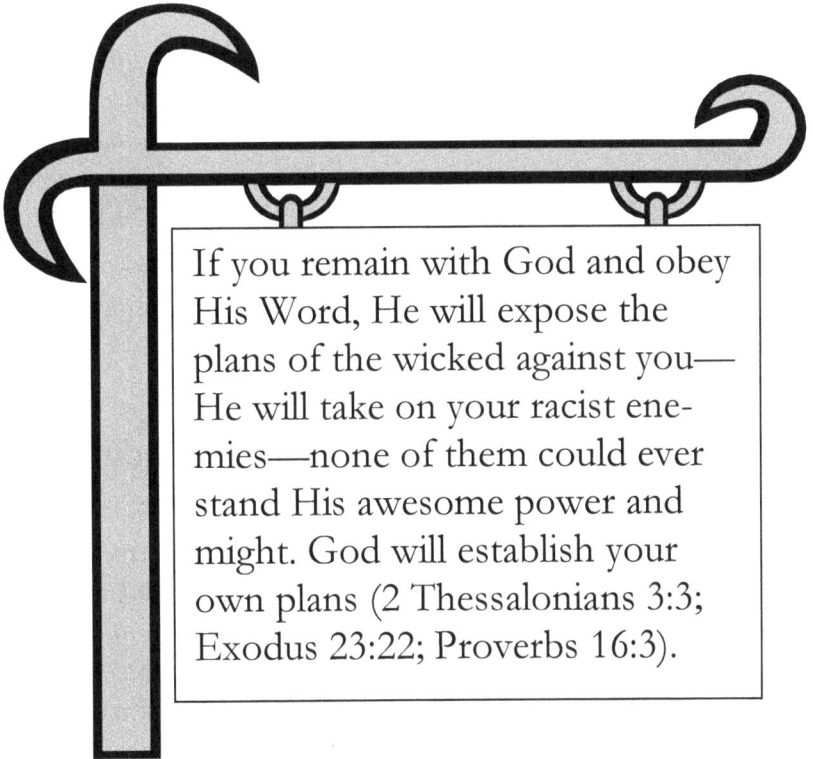

If you remain with God and obey His Word, He will expose the plans of the wicked against you—He will take on your racist enemies—none of them could ever stand His awesome power and might. God will establish your own plans (2 Thessalonians 3:3; Exodus 23:22; Proverbs 16:3).

108

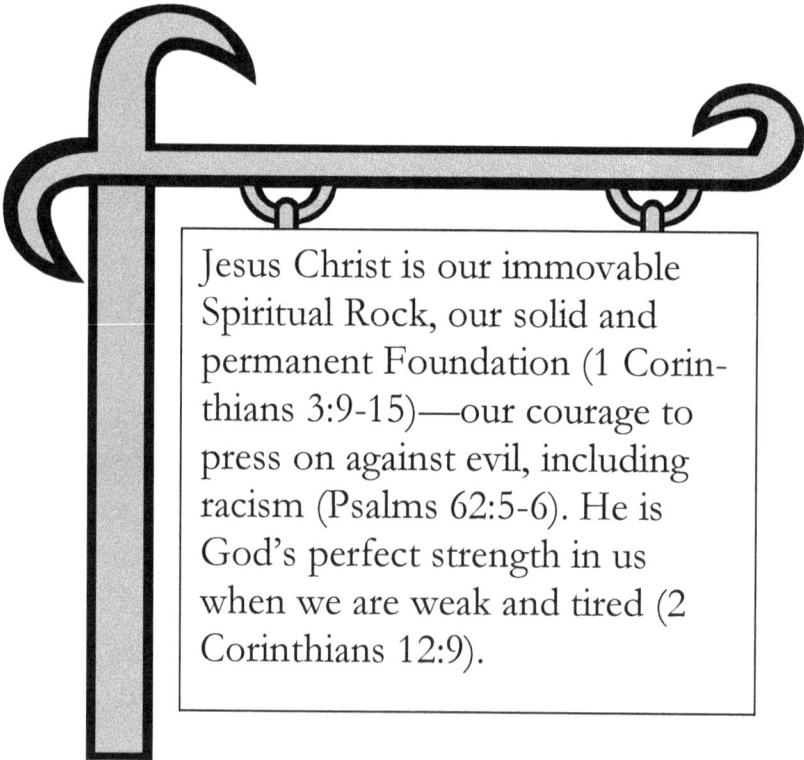

Jesus Christ is our immovable Spiritual Rock, our solid and permanent Foundation (1 Corinthians 3:9-15)—our courage to press on against evil, including racism (Psalms 62:5-6). He is God's perfect strength in us when we are weak and tired (2 Corinthians 12:9).

109

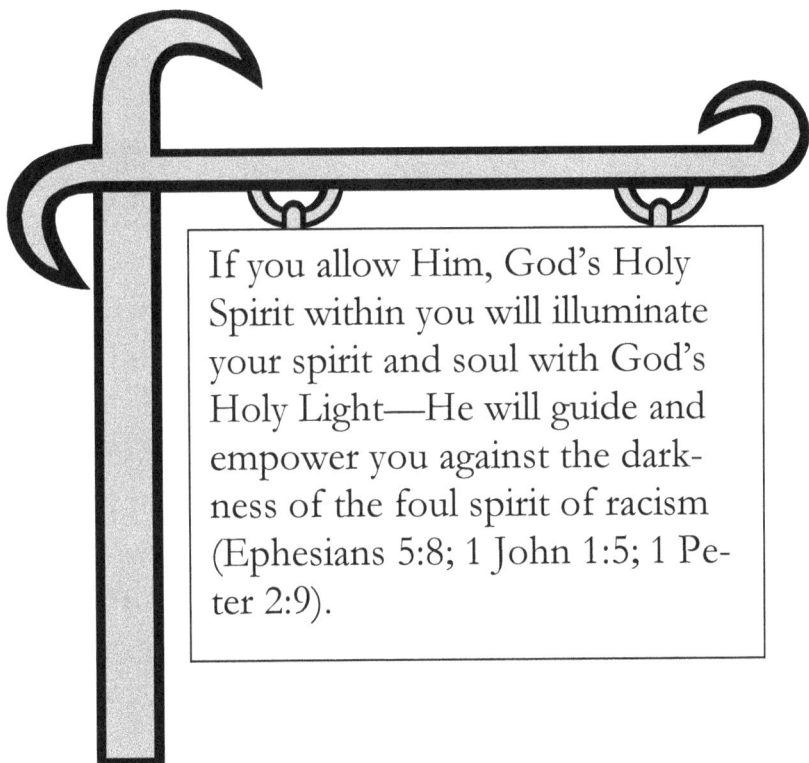

If you allow Him, God's Holy Spirit within you will illuminate your spirit and soul with God's Holy Light—He will guide and empower you against the darkness of the foul spirit of racism (Ephesians 5:8; 1 John 1:5; 1 Peter 2:9).

110

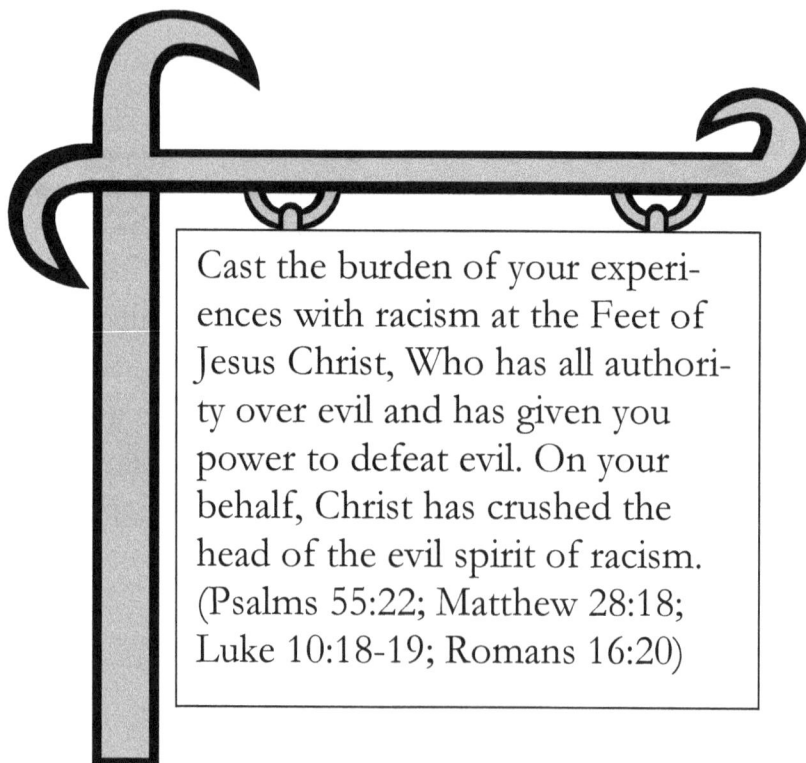

Cast the burden of your experiences with racism at the Feet of Jesus Christ, Who has all authority over evil and has given you power to defeat evil. On your behalf, Christ has crushed the head of the evil spirit of racism. (Psalms 55:22; Matthew 28:18; Luke 10:18-19; Romans 16:20)

111

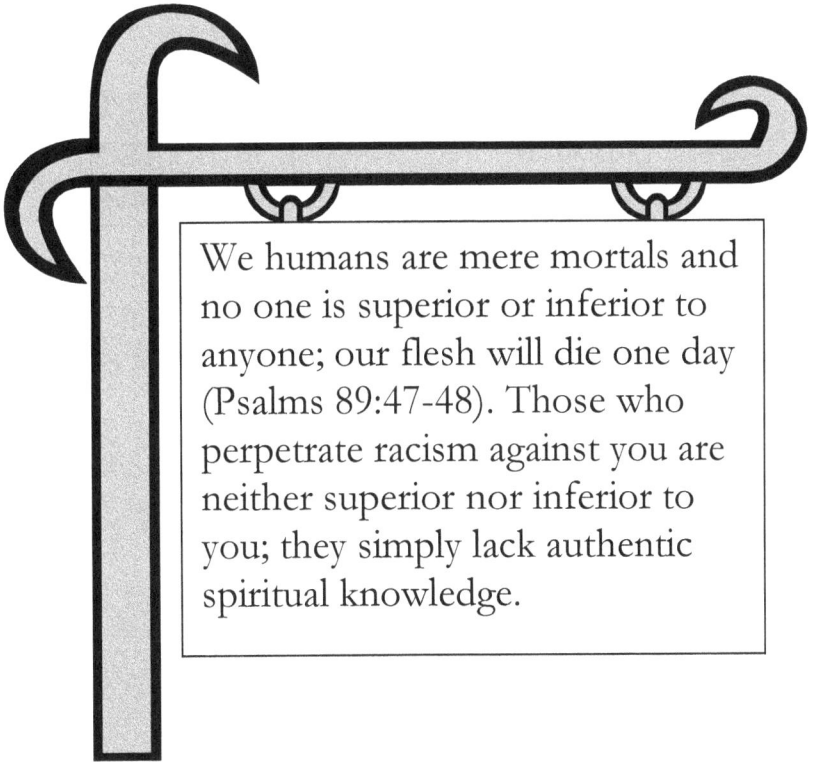

We humans are mere mortals and no one is superior or inferior to anyone; our flesh will die one day (Psalms 89:47-48). Those who perpetrate racism against you are neither superior nor inferior to you; they simply lack authentic spiritual knowledge.

112

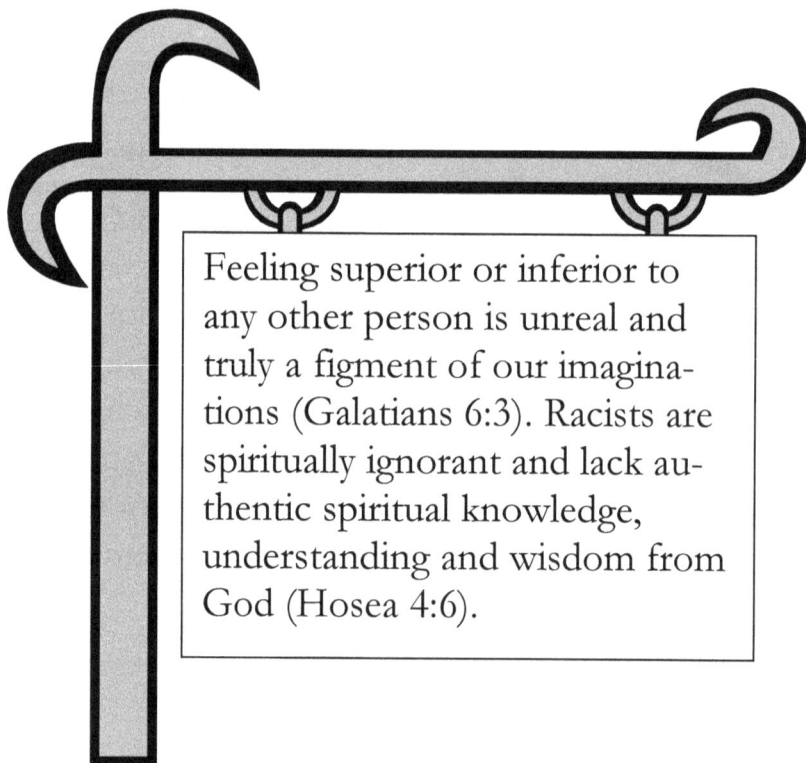

Feeling superior or inferior to any other person is unreal and truly a figment of our imaginations (Galatians 6:3). Racists are spiritually ignorant and lack authentic spiritual knowledge, understanding and wisdom from God (Hosea 4:6).

113

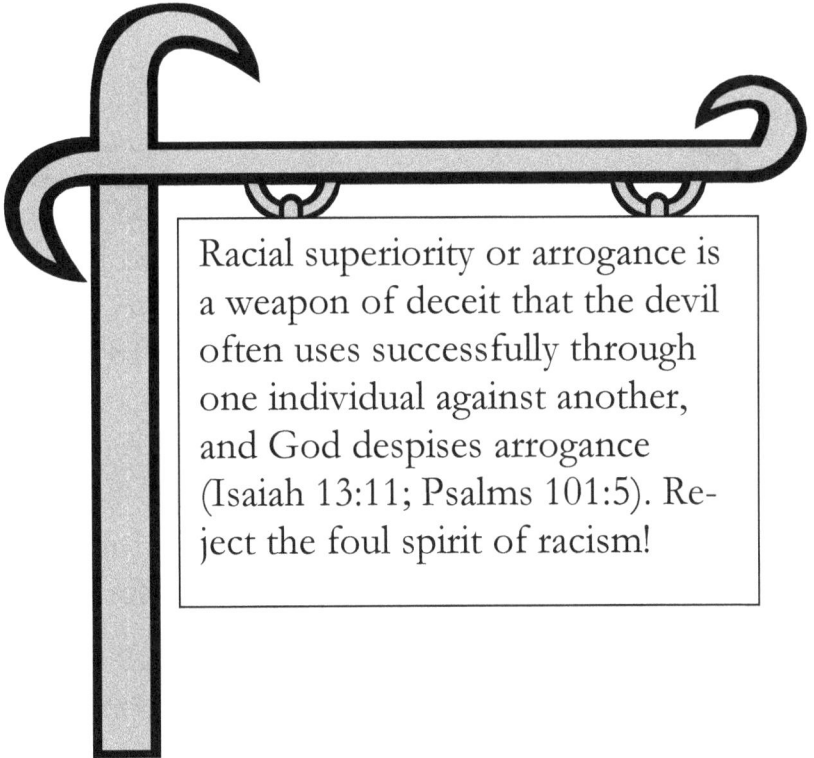

Racial superiority or arrogance is a weapon of deceit that the devil often uses successfully through one individual against another, and God despises arrogance (Isaiah 13:11; Psalms 101:5). Reject the foul spirit of racism!

114

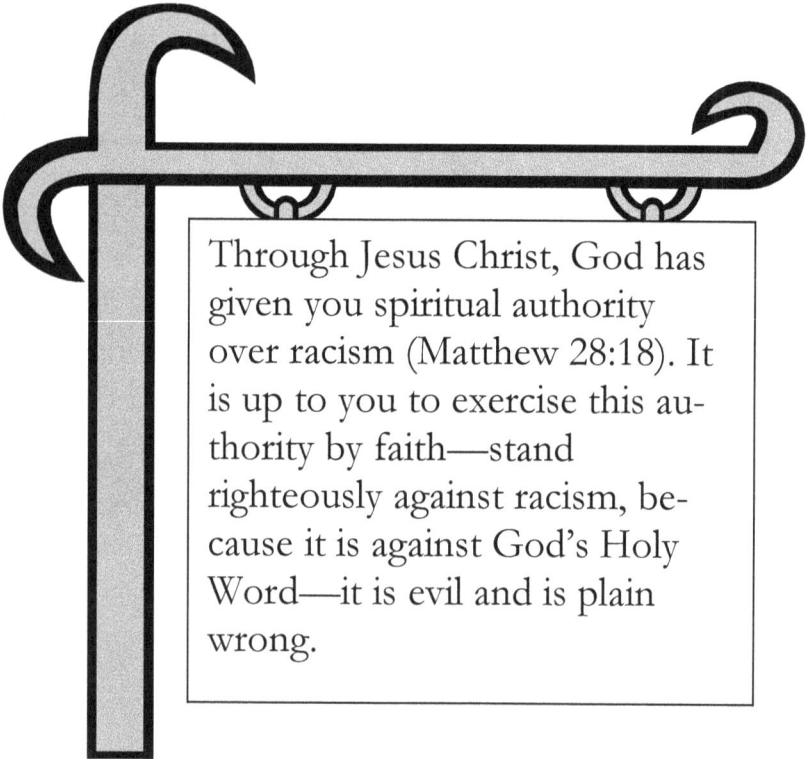

Through Jesus Christ, God has given you spiritual authority over racism (Matthew 28:18). It is up to you to exercise this authority by faith—stand righteously against racism, because it is against God's Holy Word—it is evil and is plain wrong.

115

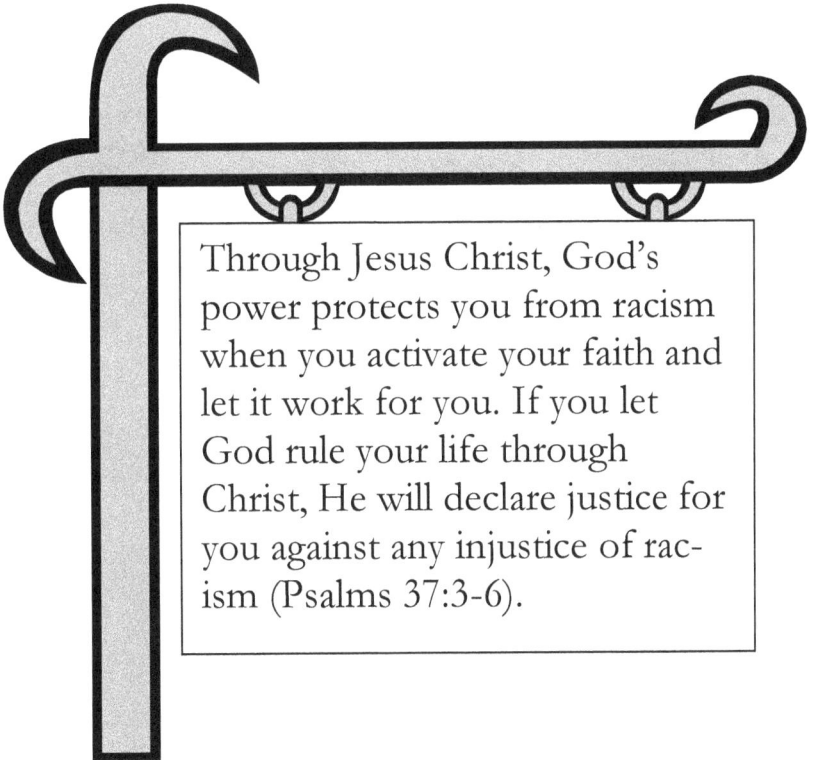

Through Jesus Christ, God's power protects you from racism when you activate your faith and let it work for you. If you let God rule your life through Christ, He will declare justice for you against any injustice of racism (Psalms 37:3-6).

116

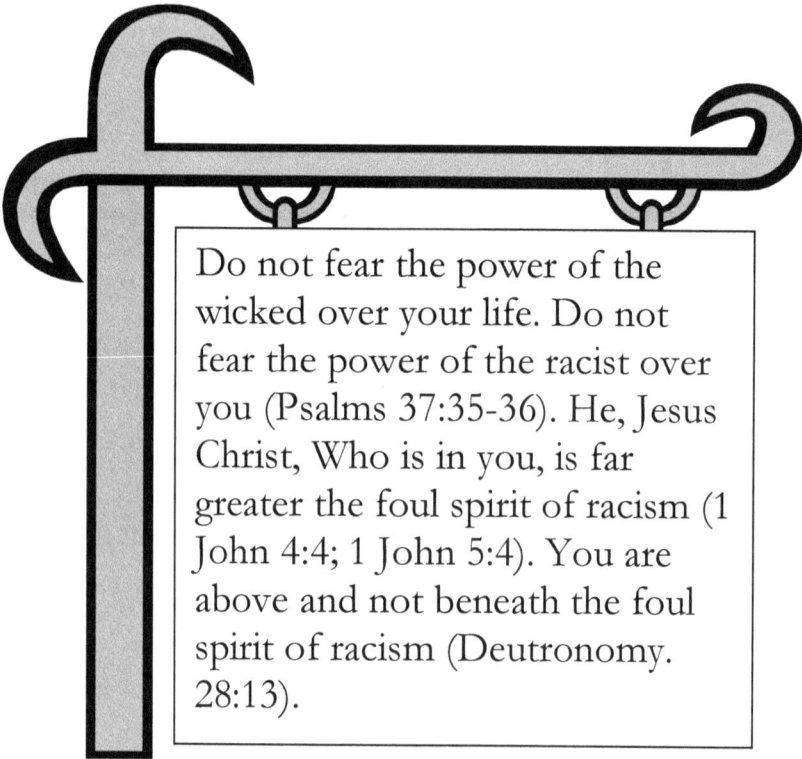

Do not fear the power of the wicked over your life. Do not fear the power of the racist over you (Psalms 37:35-36). He, Jesus Christ, Who is in you, is far greater the foul spirit of racism (1 John 4:4; 1 John 5:4). You are above and not beneath the foul spirit of racism (Deutronomy. 28:13).

117

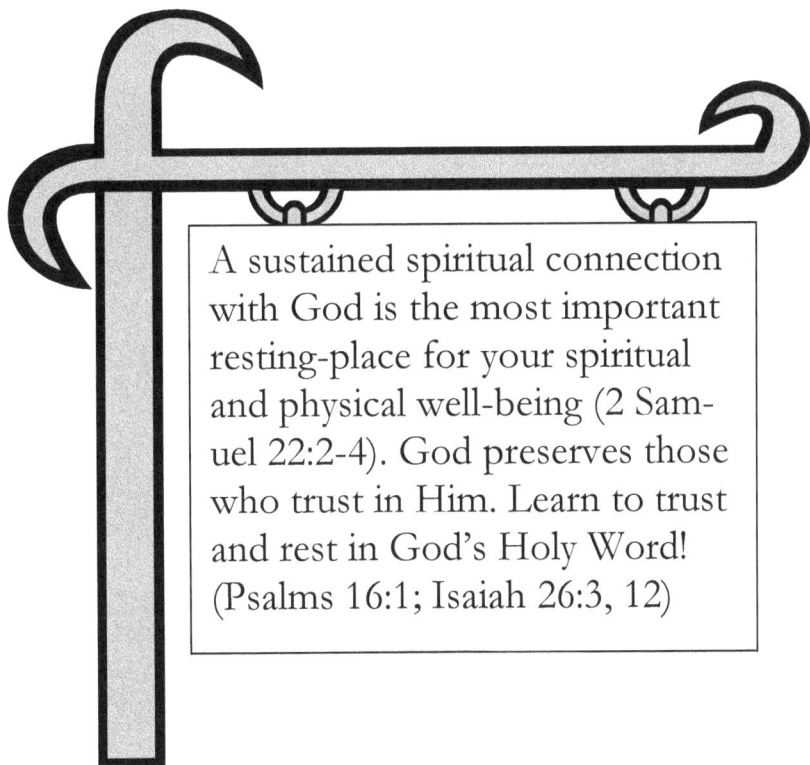

A sustained spiritual connection with God is the most important resting-place for your spiritual and physical well-being (2 Samuel 22:2-4). God preserves those who trust in Him. Learn to trust and rest in God's Holy Word! (Psalms 16:1; Isaiah 26:3, 12)

118

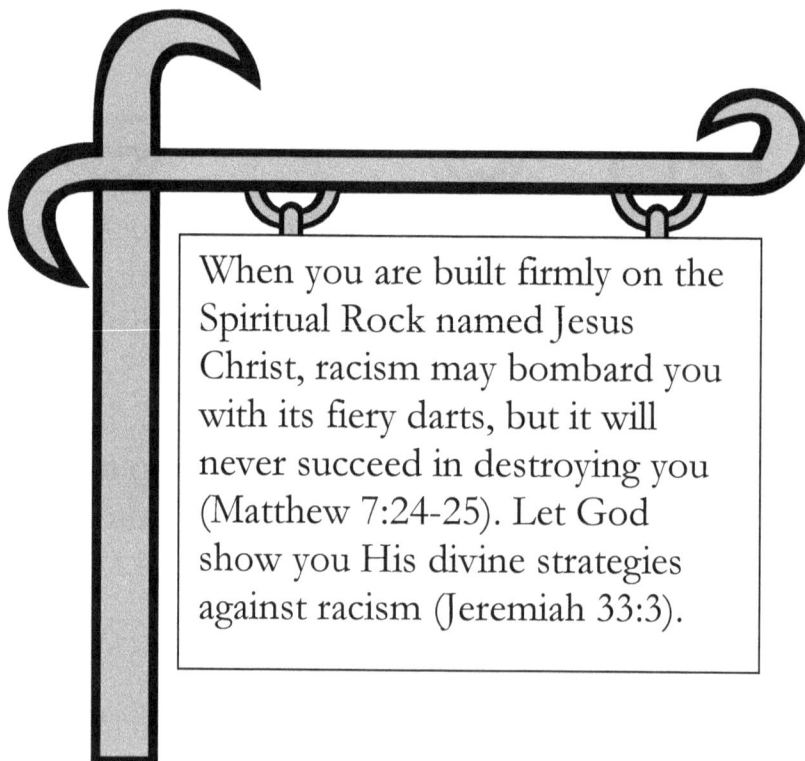

When you are built firmly on the Spiritual Rock named Jesus Christ, racism may bombard you with its fiery darts, but it will never succeed in destroying you (Matthew 7:24-25). Let God show you His divine strategies against racism (Jeremiah 33:3).

119

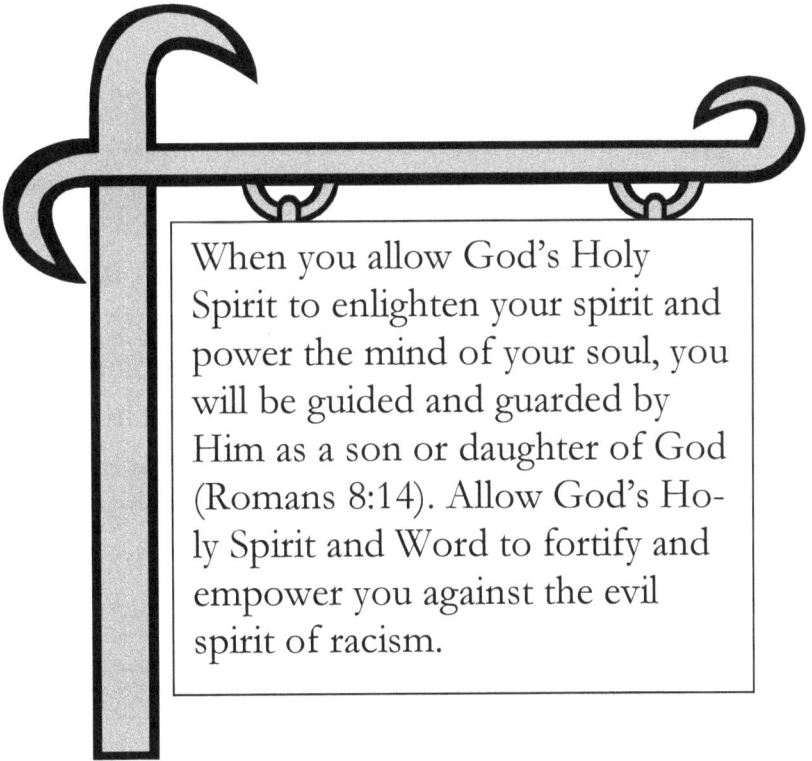

When you allow God's Holy Spirit to enlighten your spirit and power the mind of your soul, you will be guided and guarded by Him as a son or daughter of God (Romans 8:14). Allow God's Holy Spirit and Word to fortify and empower you against the evil spirit of racism.

120

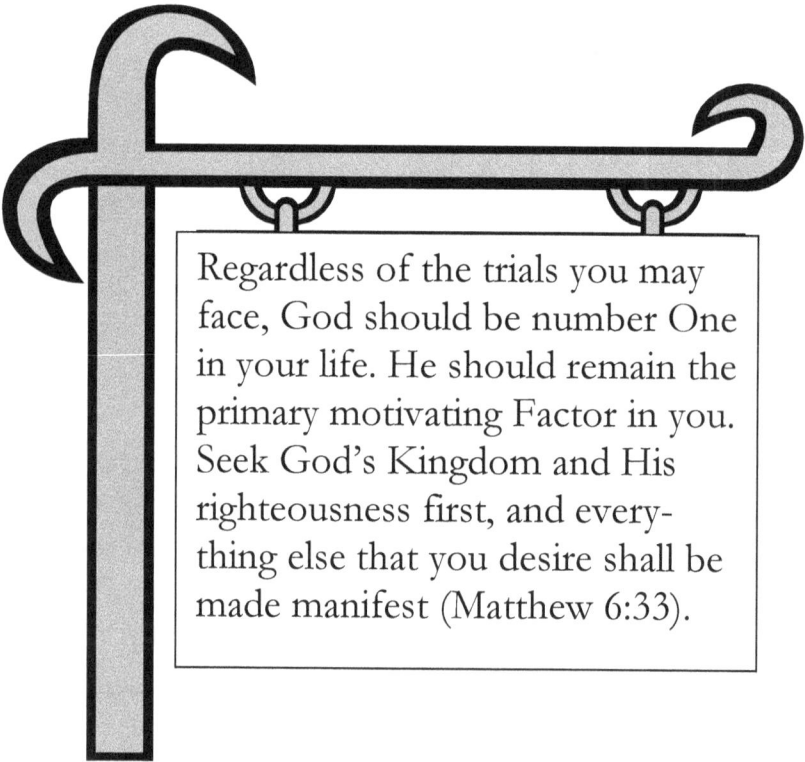

Regardless of the trials you may face, God should be number One in your life. He should remain the primary motivating Factor in you. Seek God's Kingdom and His righteousness first, and everything else that you desire shall be made manifest (Matthew 6:33).

121

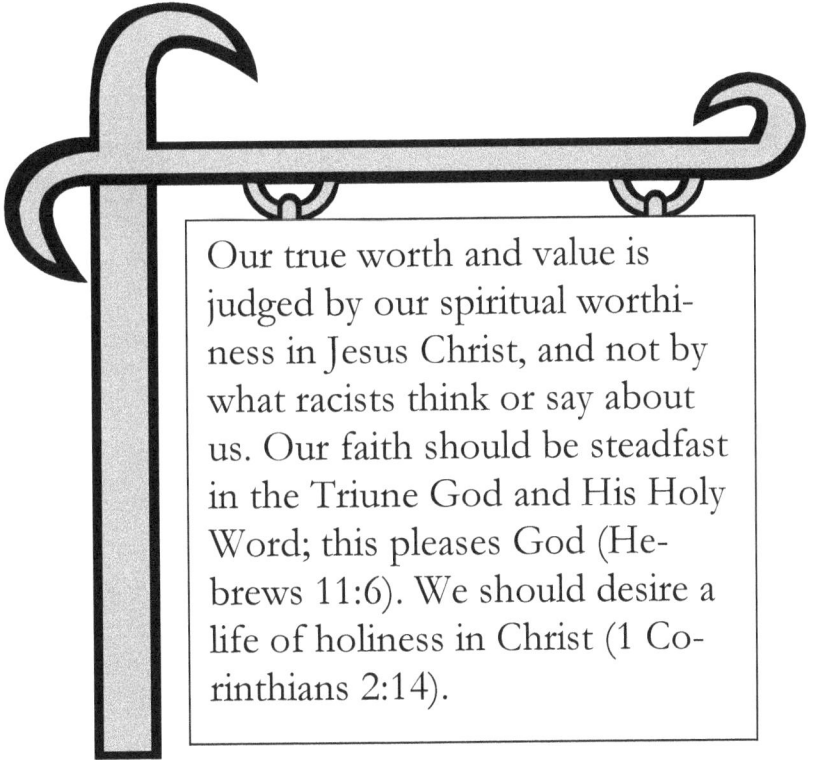

Our true worth and value is judged by our spiritual worthiness in Jesus Christ, and not by what racists think or say about us. Our faith should be steadfast in the Triune God and His Holy Word; this pleases God (Hebrews 11:6). We should desire a life of holiness in Christ (1 Corinthians 2:14).

122

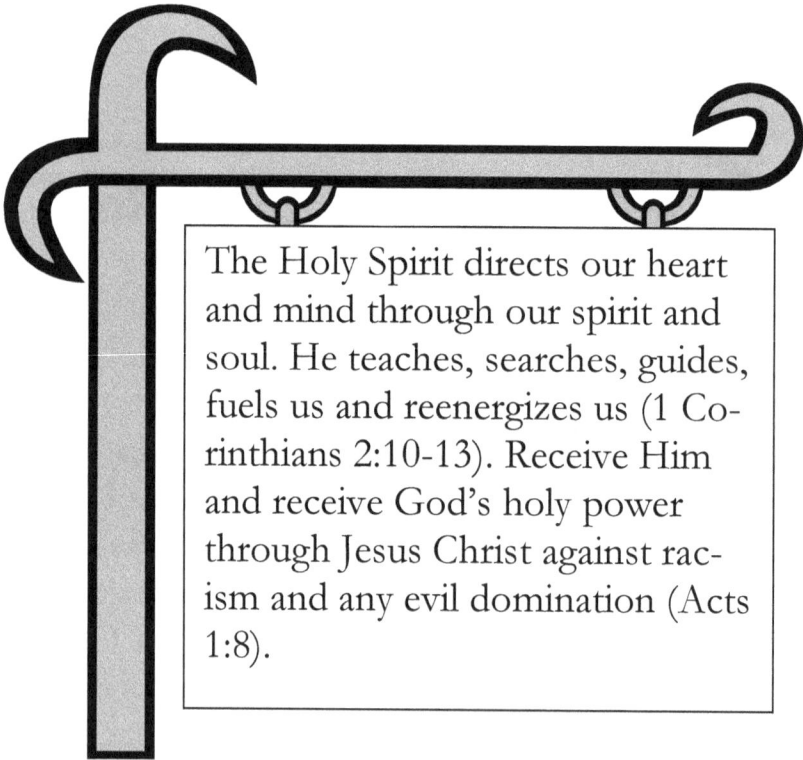

The Holy Spirit directs our heart and mind through our spirit and soul. He teaches, searches, guides, fuels us and reenergizes us (1 Corinthians 2:10-13). Receive Him and receive God's holy power through Jesus Christ against racism and any evil domination (Acts 1:8).

123

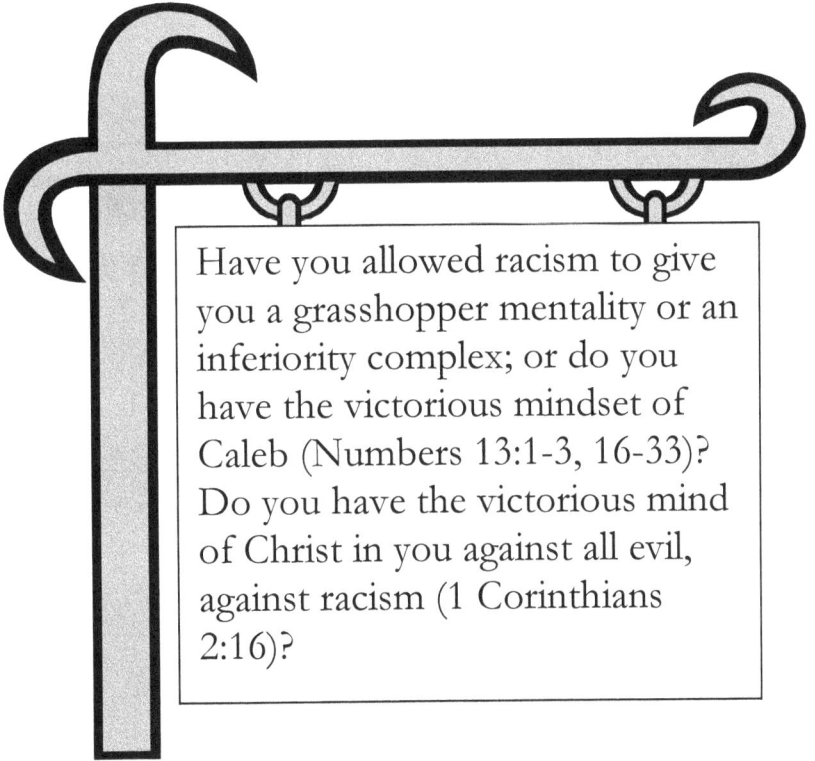

Have you allowed racism to give you a grasshopper mentality or an inferiority complex; or do you have the victorious mindset of Caleb (Numbers 13:1-3, 16-33)? Do you have the victorious mind of Christ in you against all evil, against racism (1 Corinthians 2:16)?

124

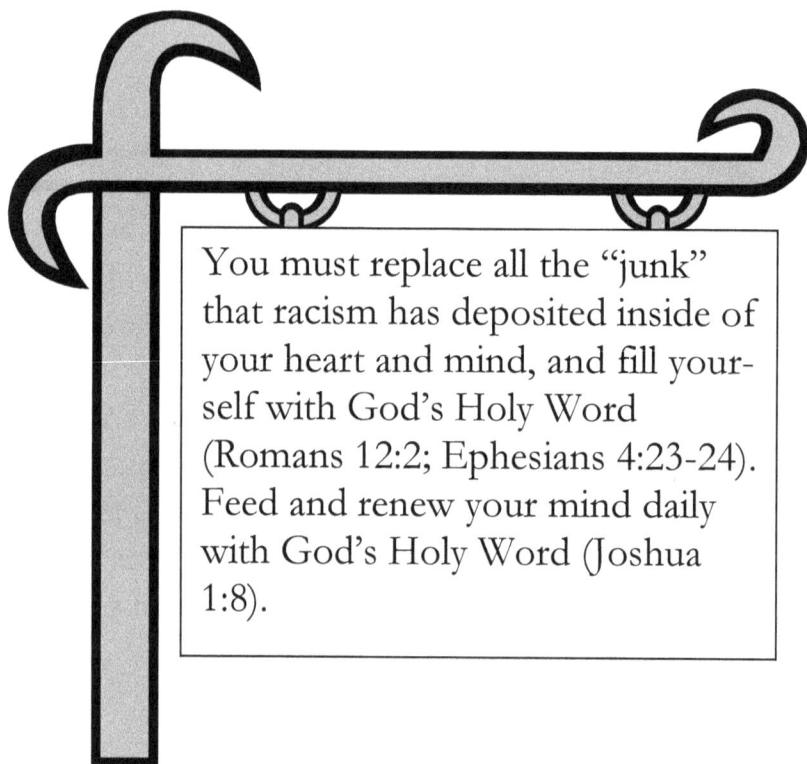

You must replace all the "junk" that racism has deposited inside of your heart and mind, and fill yourself with God's Holy Word (Romans 12:2; Ephesians 4:23-24). Feed and renew your mind daily with God's Holy Word (Joshua 1:8).

125

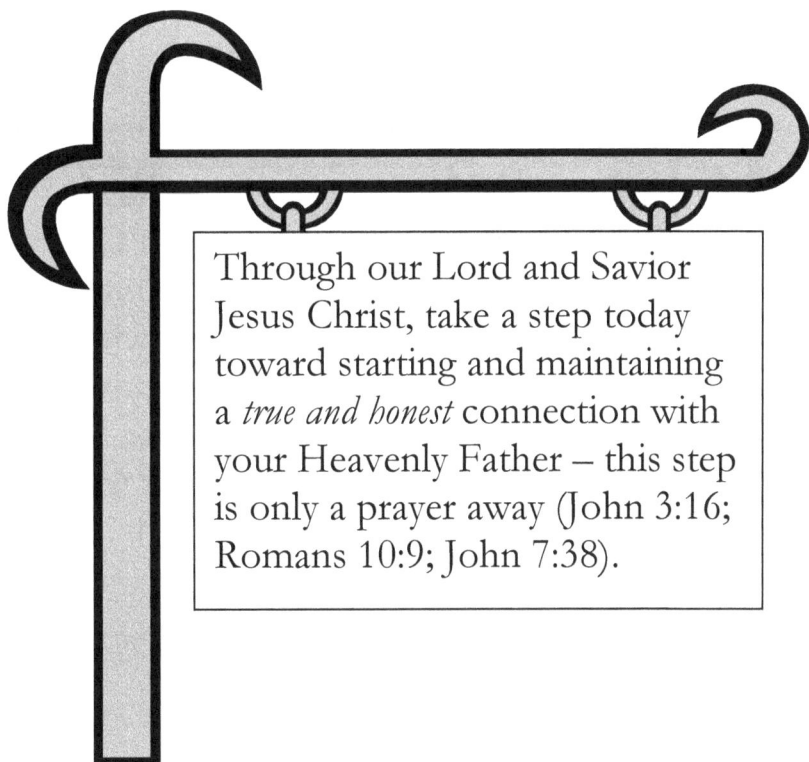

Through our Lord and Savior Jesus Christ, take a step today toward starting and maintaining a *true and honest* connection with your Heavenly Father – this step is only a prayer away (John 3:16; Romans 10:9; John 7:38).

126

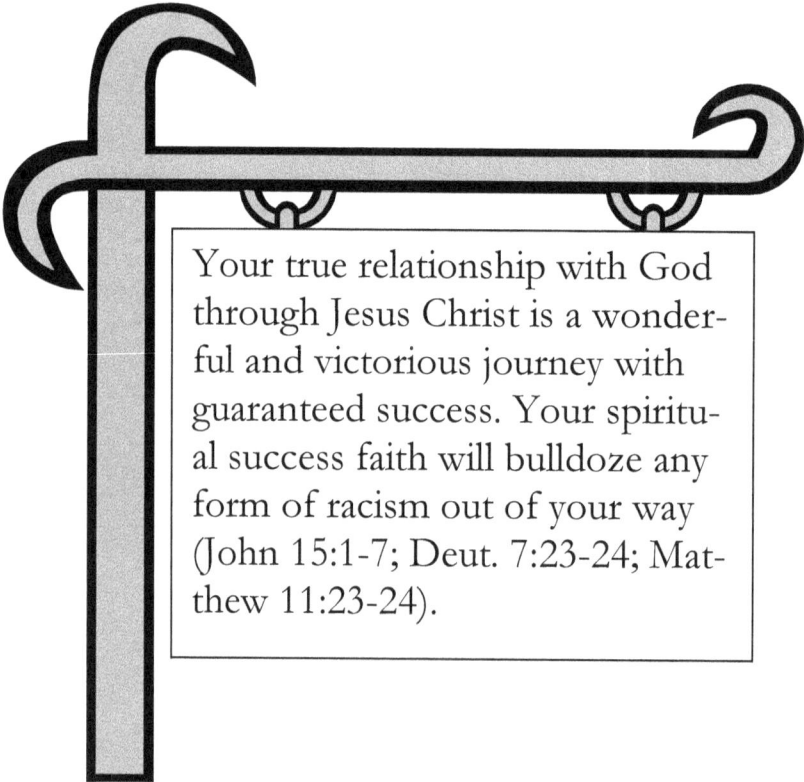

Your true relationship with God through Jesus Christ is a wonderful and victorious journey with guaranteed success. Your spiritual success faith will bulldoze any form of racism out of your way (John 15:1-7; Deut. 7:23-24; Matthew 11:23-24).

127

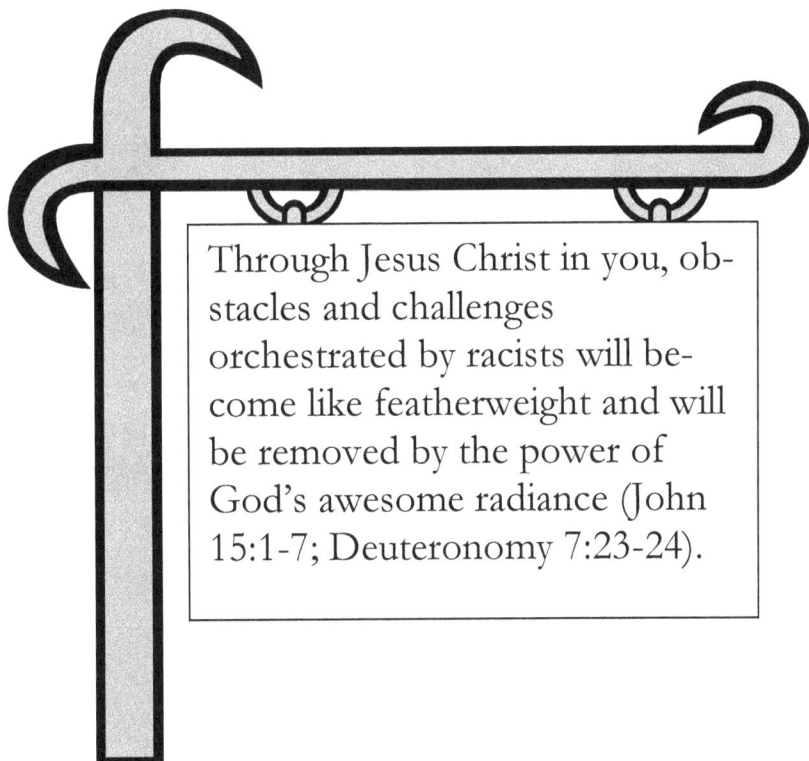

Through Jesus Christ in you, obstacles and challenges orchestrated by racists will become like featherweight and will be removed by the power of God's awesome radiance (John 15:1-7; Deuteronomy 7:23-24).

128

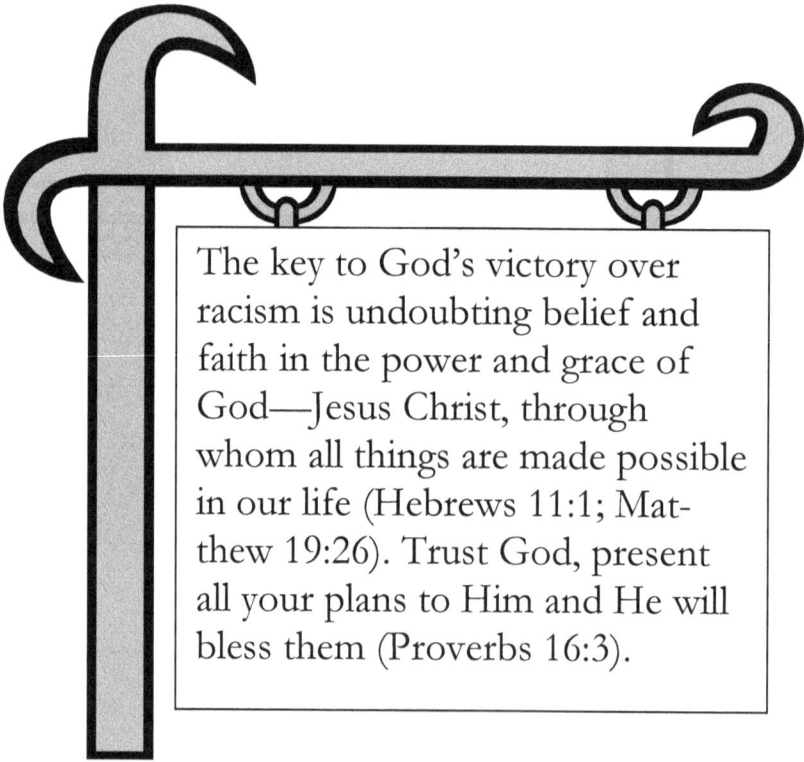

The key to God's victory over racism is undoubting belief and faith in the power and grace of God—Jesus Christ, through whom all things are made possible in our life (Hebrews 11:1; Matthew 19:26). Trust God, present all your plans to Him and He will bless them (Proverbs 16:3).

129

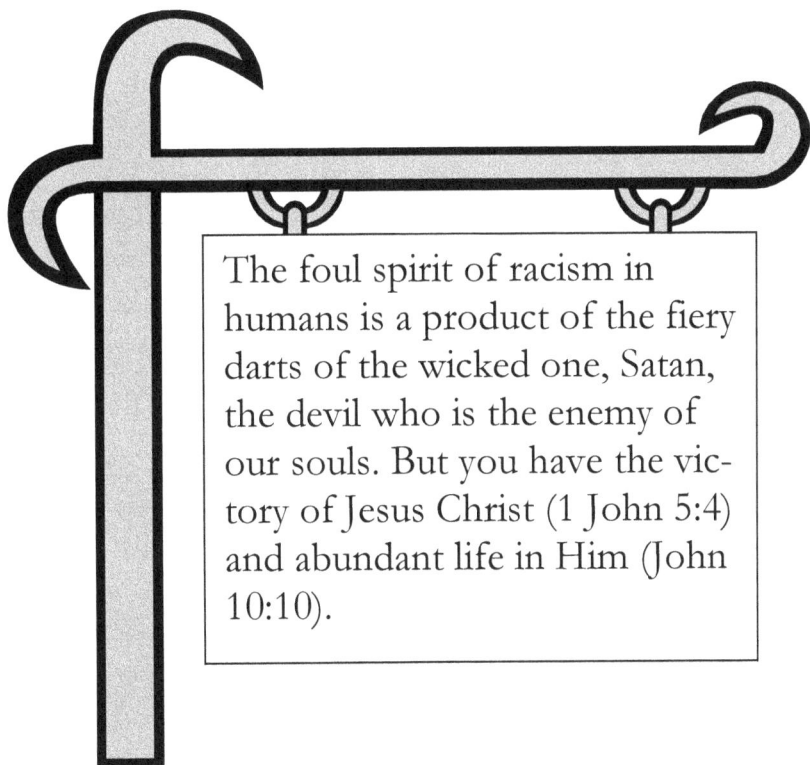

The foul spirit of racism in humans is a product of the fiery darts of the wicked one, Satan, the devil who is the enemy of our souls. But you have the victory of Jesus Christ (1 John 5:4) and abundant life in Him (John 10:10).

130

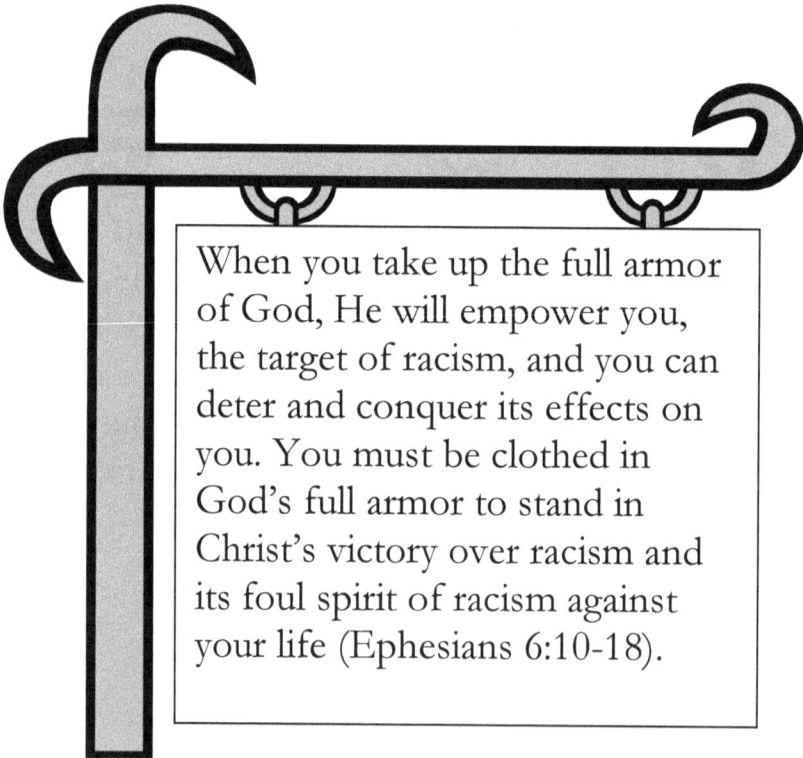

When you take up the full armor of God, He will empower you, the target of racism, and you can deter and conquer its effects on you. You must be clothed in God's full armor to stand in Christ's victory over racism and its foul spirit of racism against your life (Ephesians 6:10-18).

131

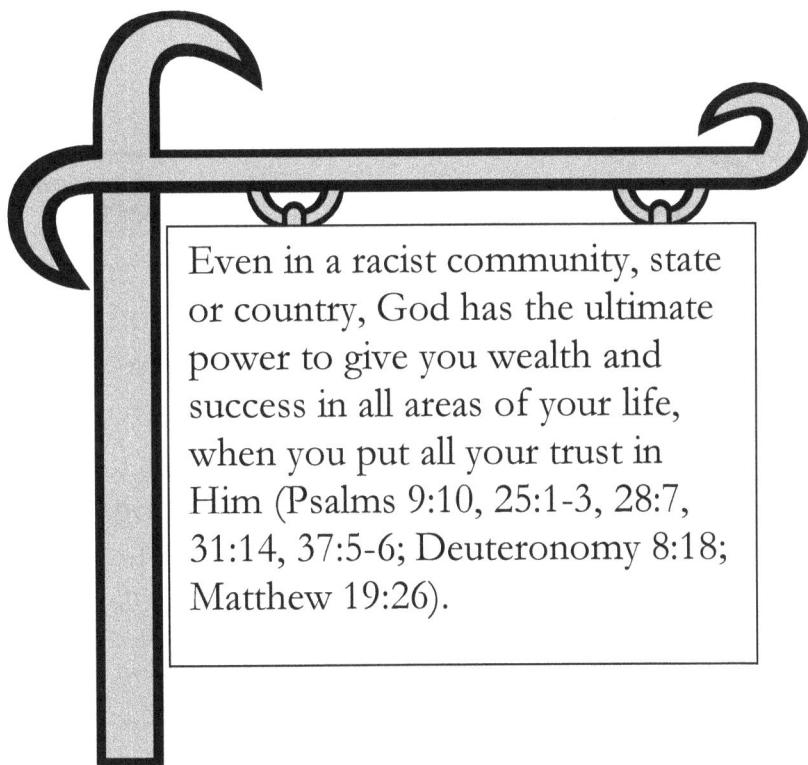

Even in a racist community, state or country, God has the ultimate power to give you wealth and success in all areas of your life, when you put all your trust in Him (Psalms 9:10, 25:1-3, 28:7, 31:14, 37:5-6; Deuteronomy 8:18; Matthew 19:26).

132

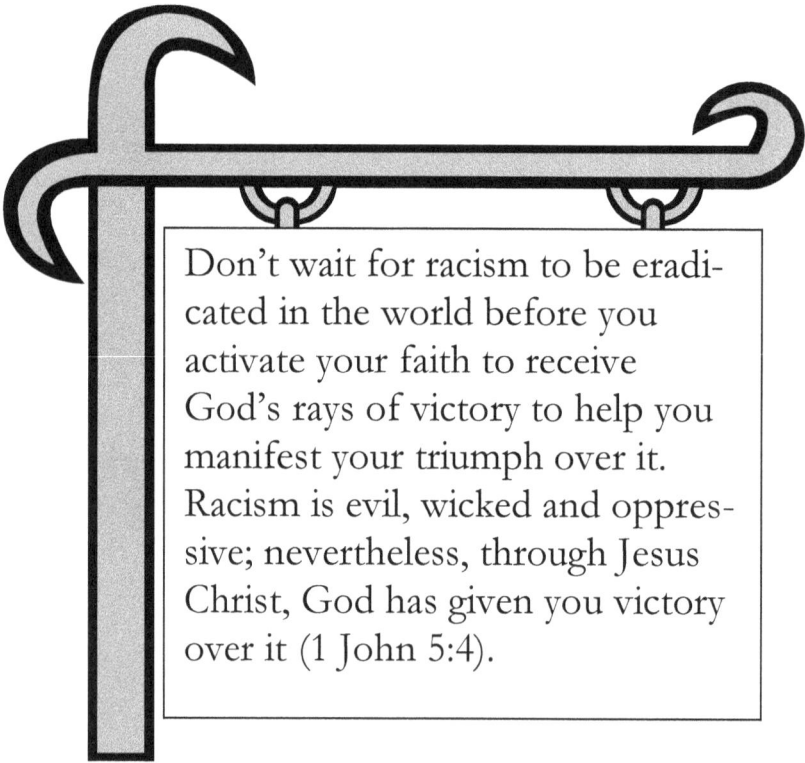

Don't wait for racism to be eradicated in the world before you activate your faith to receive God's rays of victory to help you manifest your triumph over it. Racism is evil, wicked and oppressive; nevertheless, through Jesus Christ, God has given you victory over it (1 John 5:4).

133

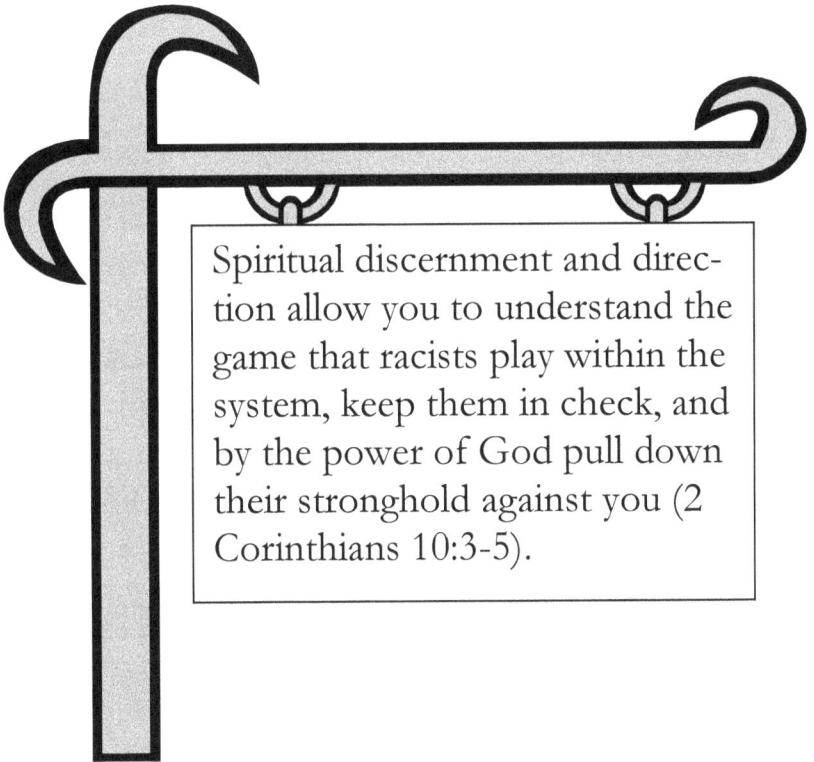

Spiritual discernment and direction allow you to understand the game that racists play within the system, keep them in check, and by the power of God pull down their stronghold against you (2 Corinthians 10:3-5).

134

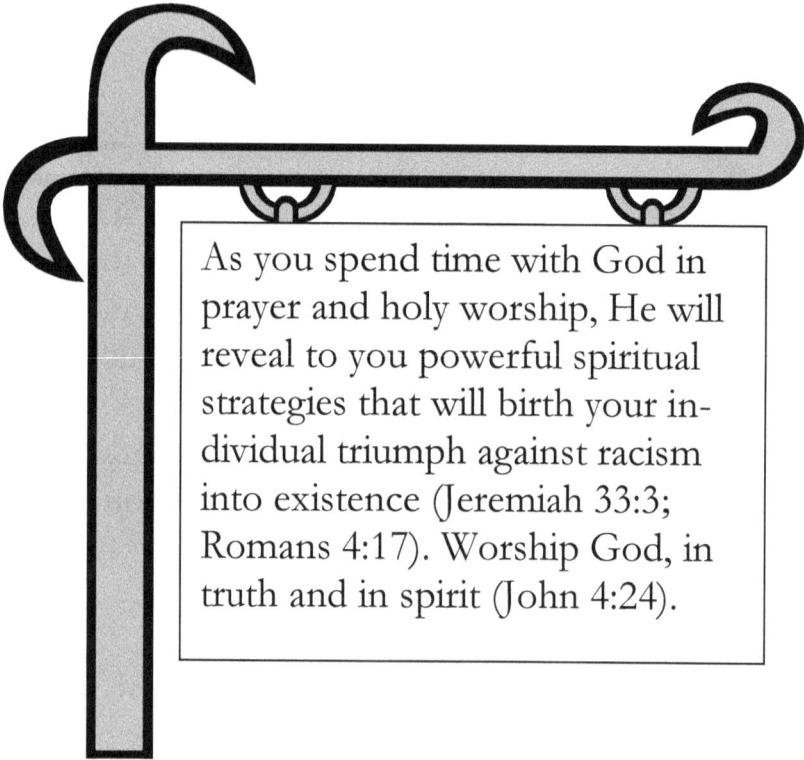

As you spend time with God in prayer and holy worship, He will reveal to you powerful spiritual strategies that will birth your individual triumph against racism into existence (Jeremiah 33:3; Romans 4:17). Worship God, in truth and in spirit (John 4:24).

135

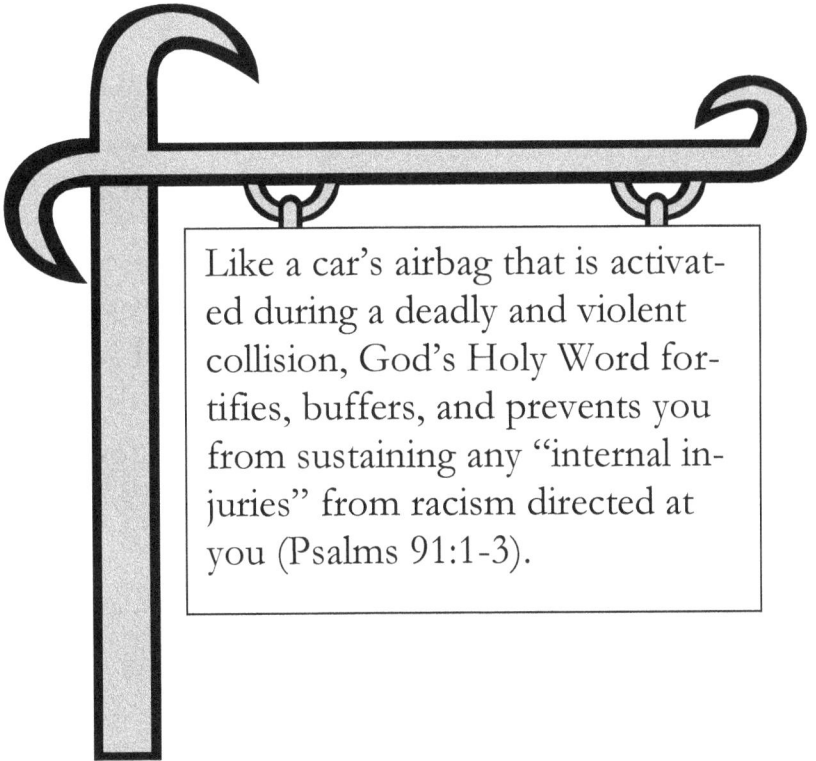

Like a car's airbag that is activated during a deadly and violent collision, God's Holy Word fortifies, buffers, and prevents you from sustaining any "internal injuries" from racism directed at you (Psalms 91:1-3).

136

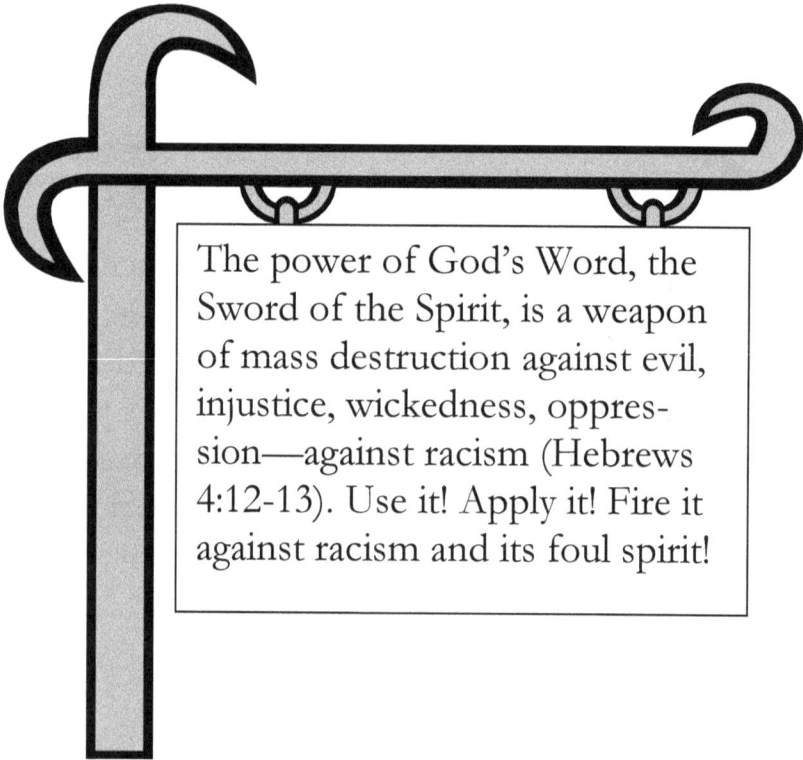

The power of God's Word, the Sword of the Spirit, is a weapon of mass destruction against evil, injustice, wickedness, oppression—against racism (Hebrews 4:12-13). Use it! Apply it! Fire it against racism and its foul spirit!

137

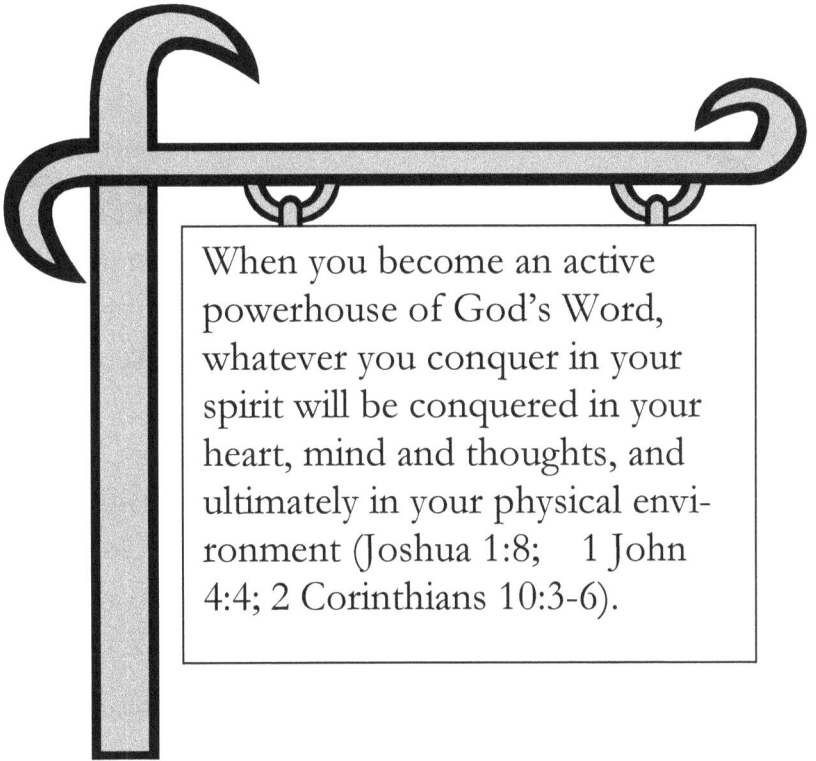

When you become an active powerhouse of God's Word, whatever you conquer in your spirit will be conquered in your heart, mind and thoughts, and ultimately in your physical environment (Joshua 1:8; 1 John 4:4; 2 Corinthians 10:3-6).

138

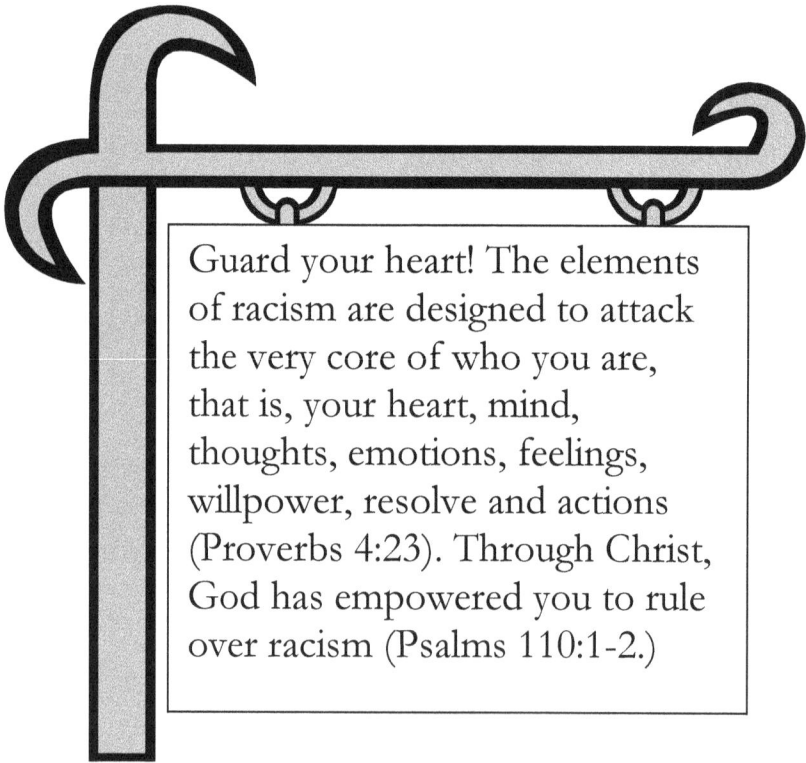

Guard your heart! The elements of racism are designed to attack the very core of who you are, that is, your heart, mind, thoughts, emotions, feelings, willpower, resolve and actions (Proverbs 4:23). Through Christ, God has empowered you to rule over racism (Psalms 110:1-2.)

139

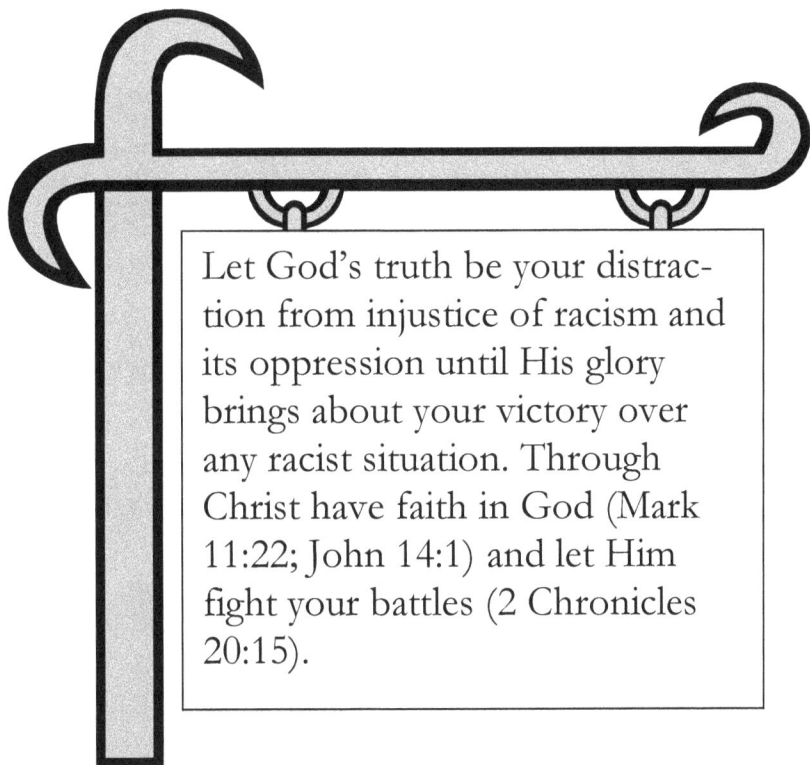

Let God's truth be your distraction from injustice of racism and its oppression until His glory brings about your victory over any racist situation. Through Christ have faith in God (Mark 11:22; John 14:1) and let Him fight your battles (2 Chronicles 20:15).

140

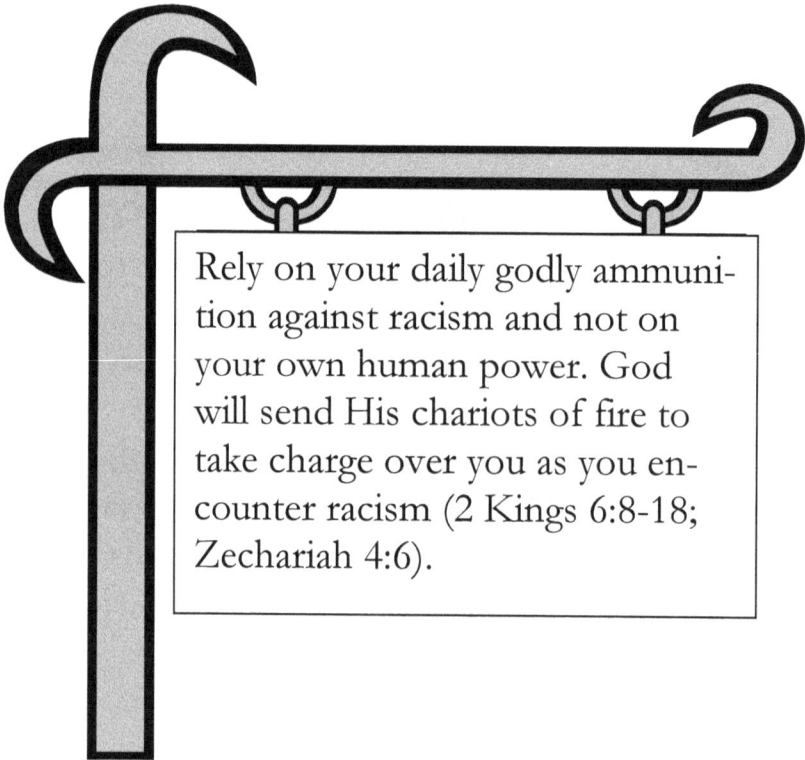

Rely on your daily godly ammunition against racism and not on your own human power. God will send His chariots of fire to take charge over you as you encounter racism (2 Kings 6:8-18; Zechariah 4:6).

141

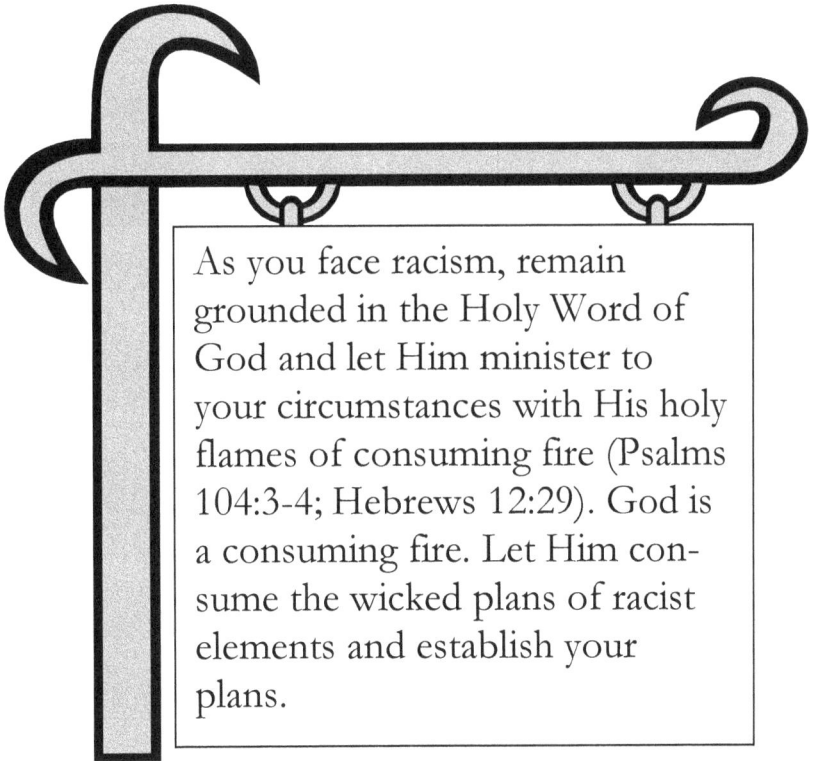

As you face racism, remain grounded in the Holy Word of God and let Him minister to your circumstances with His holy flames of consuming fire (Psalms 104:3-4; Hebrews 12:29). God is a consuming fire. Let Him consume the wicked plans of racist elements and establish your plans.

142

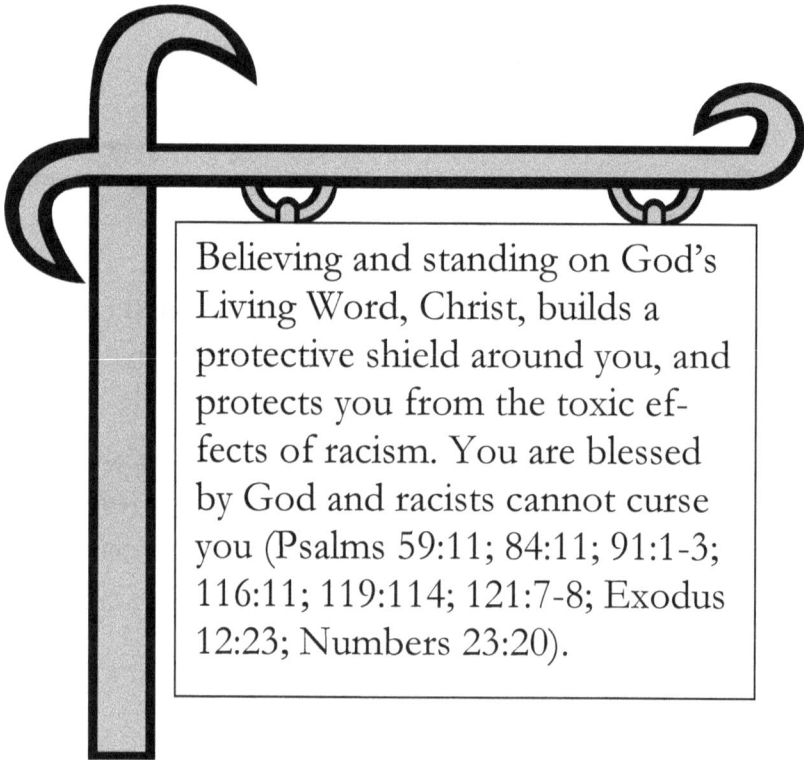

Believing and standing on God's Living Word, Christ, builds a protective shield around you, and protects you from the toxic effects of racism. You are blessed by God and racists cannot curse you (Psalms 59:11; 84:11; 91:1-3; 116:11; 119:114; 121:7-8; Exodus 12:23; Numbers 23:20).

143

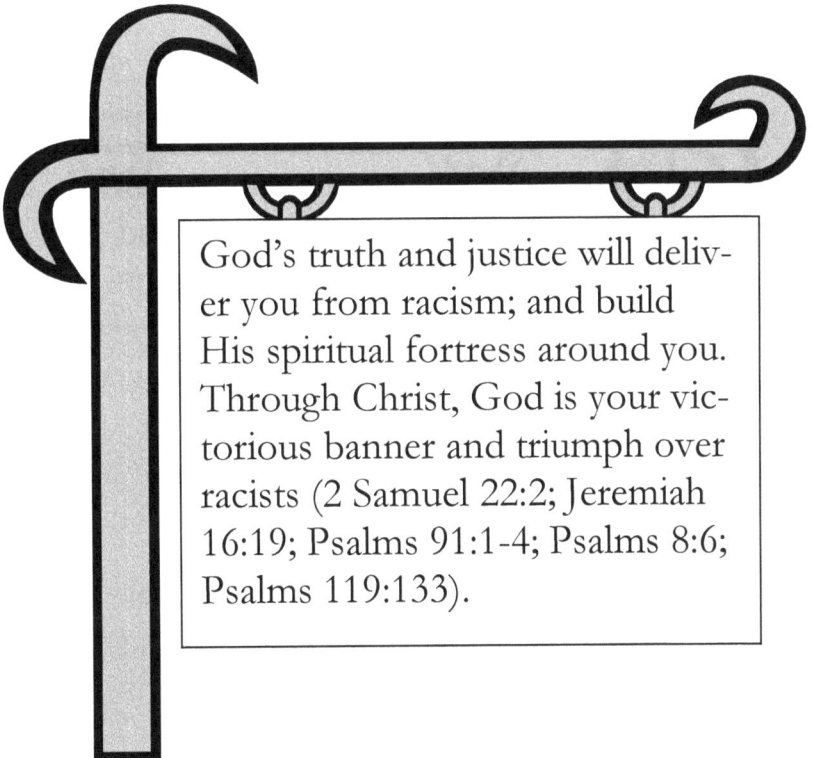

God's truth and justice will deliver you from racism; and build His spiritual fortress around you. Through Christ, God is your victorious banner and triumph over racists (2 Samuel 22:2; Jeremiah 16:19; Psalms 91:1-4; Psalms 8:6; Psalms 119:133).

144

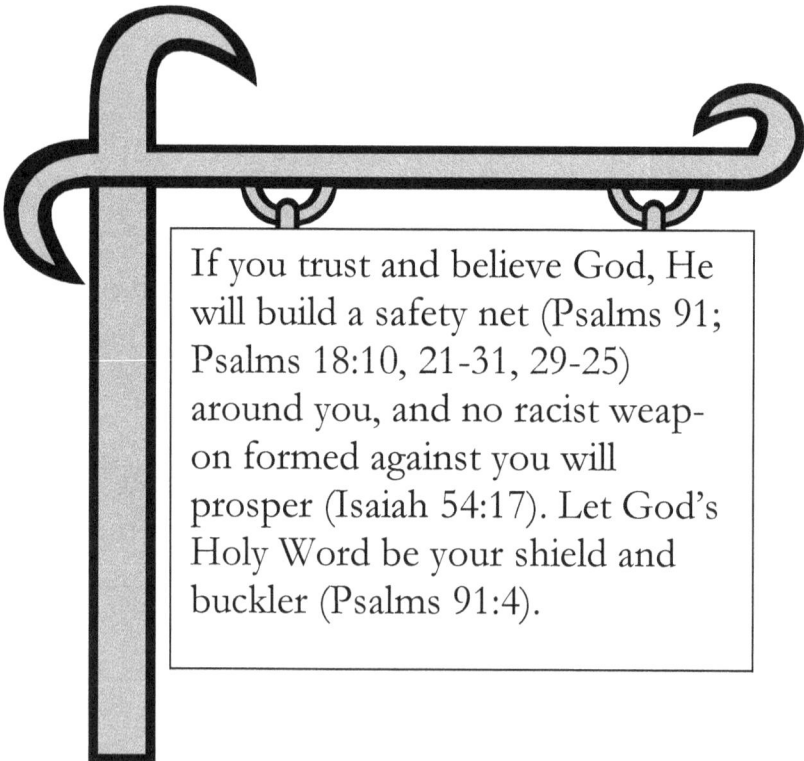

If you trust and believe God, He will build a safety net (Psalms 91; Psalms 18:10, 21-31, 29-25) around you, and no racist weapon formed against you will prosper (Isaiah 54:17). Let God's Holy Word be your shield and buckler (Psalms 91:4).

145

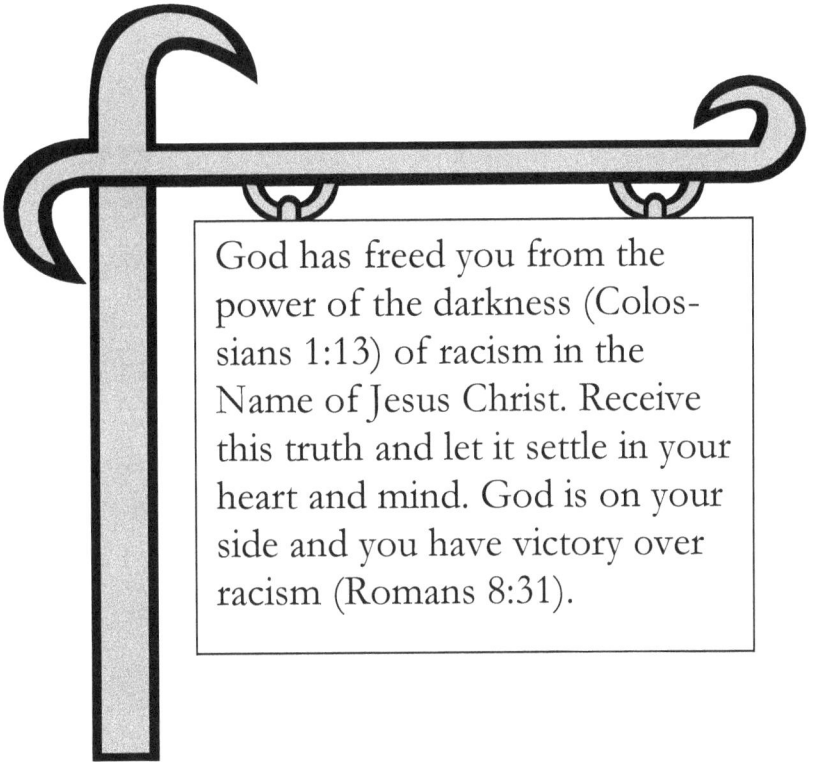

God has freed you from the power of the darkness (Colossians 1:13) of racism in the Name of Jesus Christ. Receive this truth and let it settle in your heart and mind. God is on your side and you have victory over racism (Romans 8:31).

146

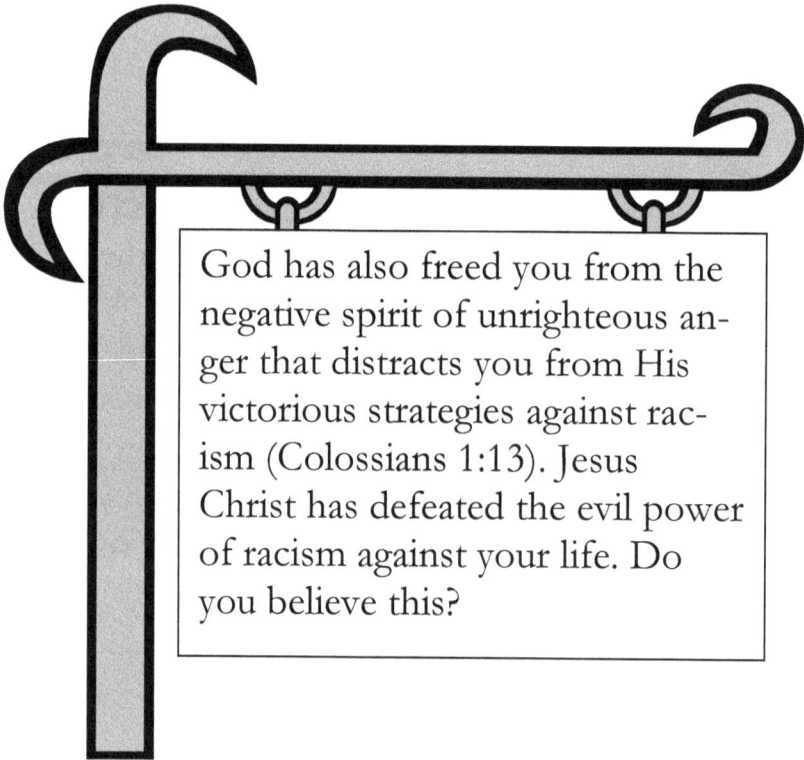

God has also freed you from the negative spirit of unrighteous anger that distracts you from His victorious strategies against racism (Colossians 1:13). Jesus Christ has defeated the evil power of racism against your life. Do you believe this?

147

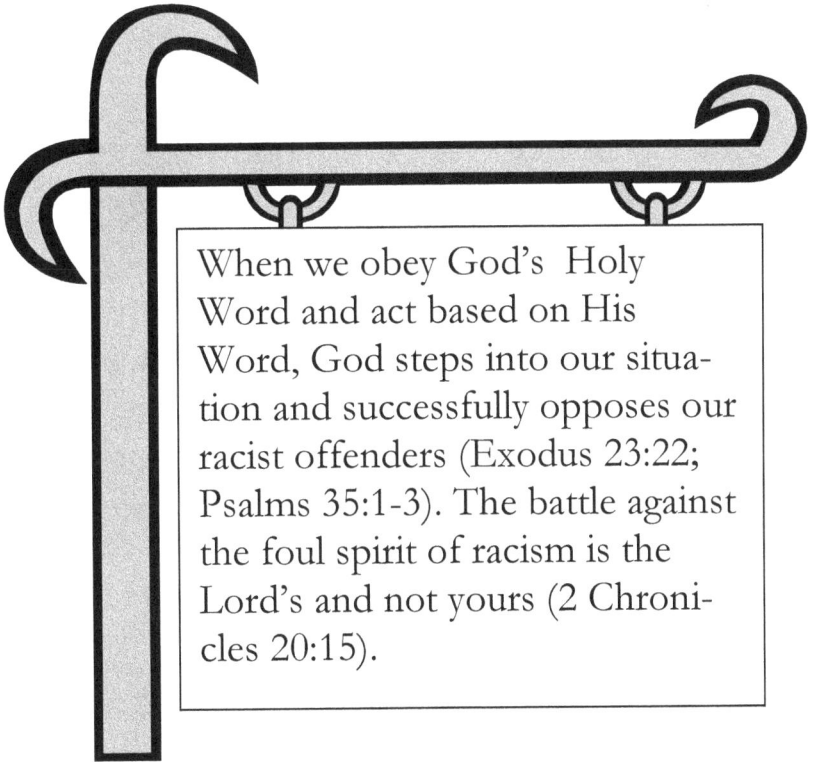

When we obey God's Holy Word and act based on His Word, God steps into our situation and successfully opposes our racist offenders (Exodus 23:22; Psalms 35:1-3). The battle against the foul spirit of racism is the Lord's and not yours (2 Chronicles 20:15).

148

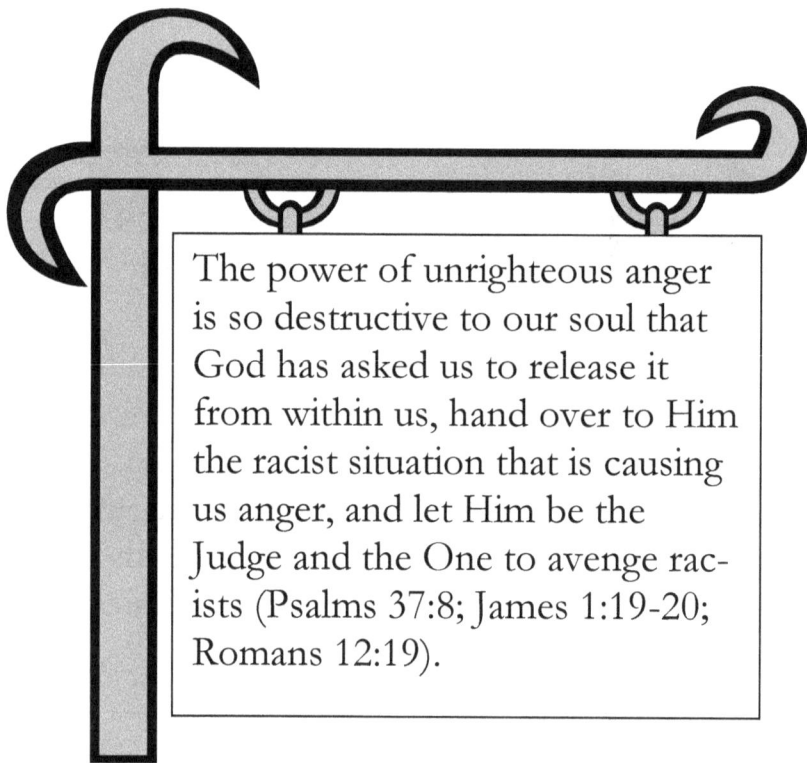

The power of unrighteous anger is so destructive to our soul that God has asked us to release it from within us, hand over to Him the racist situation that is causing us anger, and let Him be the Judge and the One to avenge racists (Psalms 37:8; James 1:19-20; Romans 12:19).

149

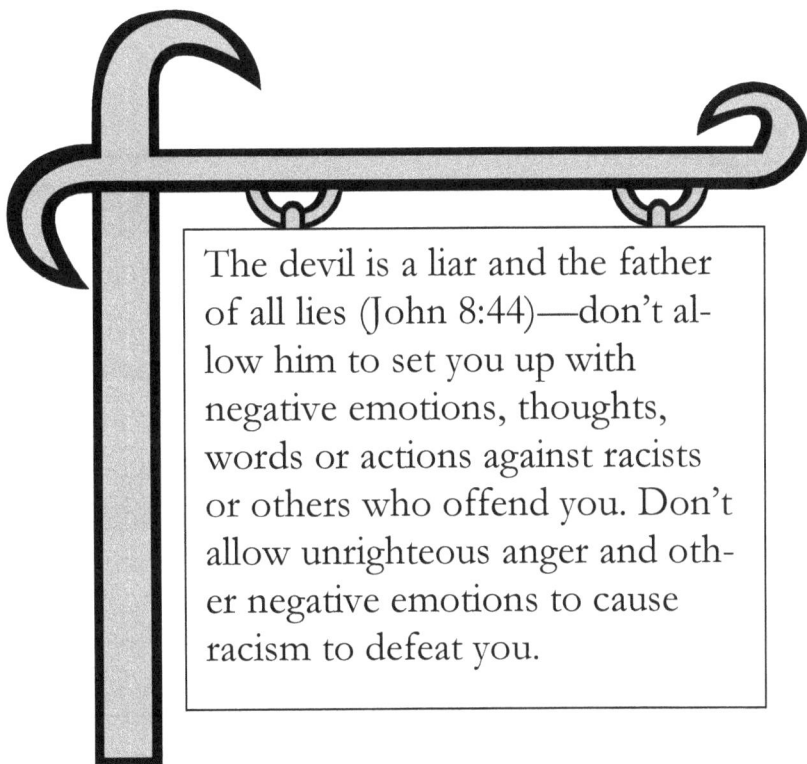

The devil is a liar and the father of all lies (John 8:44)—don't allow him to set you up with negative emotions, thoughts, words or actions against racists or others who offend you. Don't allow unrighteous anger and other negative emotions to cause racism to defeat you.

150

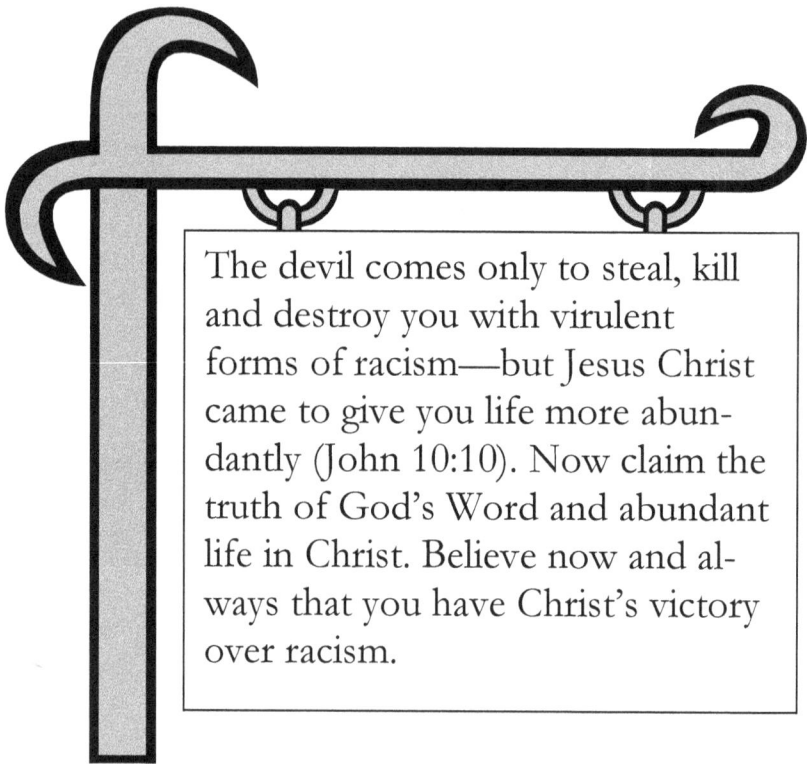

The devil comes only to steal, kill and destroy you with virulent forms of racism—but Jesus Christ came to give you life more abundantly (John 10:10). Now claim the truth of God's Word and abundant life in Christ. Believe now and always that you have Christ's victory over racism.

∞∞∞∞∞∞∞∞∞ ♦ ♦ ♦ ♦ ♦ ∞∞∞∞∞∞∞∞∞

"Keep thy heart with all diligence; for out of it are the issues of life."

Proverbs 4:23

∞∞∞∞∞∞∞∞∞ ♦ ♦ ♦ ♦ ♦ ∞∞∞∞∞∞∞∞∞

Available:

RAYS OF VICTORY SERIES

This Book is:

150 SIGN POSTS TO VICTORY OVER RACISM
(Volume 1)

Empowering Sign Posts for Victory Over Racism

∞∞∞∞∞∞∞∞∞ ♦ ♦ ♦ ♦ ♦ ∞∞∞∞∞∞∞∞∞

Excerpts from "Nailing Racism to the Cross"

∞∞∞∞∞∞∞∞∞ ♦ ♦ ♦ ♦ ♦ ∞∞∞∞∞∞∞∞∞

By
Dr. Jacyee Aniagolu-Johnson

First Paperback Edition
ISBN 978-1-937230-01-2

Also Available:

RAYS OF VICTORY'
SERIES

150 SIGN POSTS TO VICTORY OVER RACISM
(Volume 2)

Empowering Sign Posts for Victory Over Racism

∞∞∞∞∞∞∞∞∞ ♦ ♦ ♦ ♦ ♦ ∞∞∞∞∞∞∞∞∞

Excerpts from "Nailing Racism to the Cross"

∞∞∞∞∞∞∞∞∞ ♦ ♦ ♦ ♦ ♦ ∞∞∞∞∞∞∞∞∞

By
Dr. Jacyee Aniagolu-Johnson

First Paperback Edition
ISBN 978-1-937230-02-9

RAYS OF VICTORY SERIES

150 SIGN POSTS TO VICTORY OVER RACISM
(Volume 3)

Empowering Sign Posts for Victory Over Racism

∞∞∞∞∞∞∞∞∞∞ ♦ ♦ ♦ ♦ ∞∞∞∞∞∞∞∞∞∞

Excerpts from "Nailing Racism to the Cross"

∞∞∞∞∞∞∞∞∞∞ ♦ ♦ ♦ ♦ ∞∞∞∞∞∞∞∞∞∞

By
Dr. Jacyee Aniagolu-Johnson

First Paperback Edition
ISBN 978-1-937230-03-6

RAYS OF VICTORY SERIES

150 POWER THOUGHTS AGAINST RACISM

Power of a Christ-rooted Mindset Over Racism

∞∞∞∞∞∞∞∞∞∞ ♦ ♦ ♦ ♦ ♦ ∞∞∞∞∞∞∞∞∞∞

Excerpts from "Nailing Racism to the Cross"

∞∞∞∞∞∞∞∞∞∞ ♦ ♦ ♦ ♦ ♦ ∞∞∞∞∞∞∞∞∞∞

By
Dr. Jacyee Aniagolu-Johnson

First Paperback Edition
ISBN 978-1-937-230-00-5

RAYS OF VICTORY SERIES

POWER THOUGHTS

Diary

FOR VICTORY OVER RACISM

Journal for Power Thoughts Against Racism
[With Excerpts from "Nailing Racism to the Cross"]

By
Dr. Jacyee Aniagolu-Johnson

First Paperback Edition:
ISBN: 978-1-937230-04-3

RAYS OF VICTORY SERIES

WORKBOOK SERIES

FOOTPRINTS OF VICTORY OVER RACISM

In the Secret Place With God

(Volume 1)

Illuminating Daily Guideposts for God's Rays of Victory Over Racism

By
Dr. Jacyee Aniagolu-Johnson

First Paperback Edition
ISBN 978-0-9789669-5-9

RAYS OF VICTORY SERIES

WORKBOOK SERIES

FOOTPRINTS OF VICTORY OVER RACISM

In the Secret Place With God
(Volume 2)

Illuminating Daily Guideposts for God's Rays of
Victory Over Racism

By
Dr. Jacyee Aniagolu-Johnson

First Paperback Edition
ISBN 978-0-9789669-6-6

RAYS OF VICTORY SERIES

ON THE HAMMOCK: WITH THE SWORD OF THE SPIRIT

FOR INDIVIDUAL VICTORY OVER RACISM

A Meditation Journal
[40 Days of Daily Meditation]
(Volume 1)

By
Dr. Jacyee Aniagolu-Johnson

First Paperback Edition
ISBN 978-0-9789669-8-0

RAYS OF VICTORY SERIES

ON THE HAMMOCK: WITH THE OIL OF GRACE

FOR INDIVIDUAL VICTORY OVER RACISM

A Meditation Journal
[40 Days of Daily Meditation]
(Volume 2)

By
Dr. Jacyee Aniagolu-Johnson

First Paperback Edition
ISBN 978-0-9789669-9-7

RAYS OF VICTORY SERIES

ONE ON ONE WITH GOD

FOR VICTORY OVER RACISM

Daily Prayer Conversations With God for Individual Victory Over Racism

By
Dr. Jacyee Aniagolu-Johnson

First Paperback Edition:
ISBN 978-0-9789669-7-3

RAYS OF VICTORY SERIES

My Rays of Victory

BIBLE STUDY DIARY

A Unique Diary for your Signature Penmanship as you Triumph Over Racism

By
Dr. Jacyee Aniagolu-Johnson

First Paperback Edition:
ISBN: 978-0-9789669-4-2

Rays of Victory Series
Correspondence:

Please send Correspondence to:

Marble Tower Publishing

P.O. Box 1654, Laurel, Maryland 20725

OR

Submit a Contact Request Form at:

www.marbletowerpublishing.com

www.ravbookseries.com